Skinny Boy

A Young Man's Battle and Triumph Over Anorexia

Skinny Boy

A Young Man's Battle and Triumph Over Anorexia

By Gary A. Grahl, MSE, LPC, NCC

AMERICAN LEGACY MEDIA
CLEARFIELD, UTAH

Library of Congress Cataloging-in-Publication Data
    Grahl, Gary A., 1968-
      Skinny boy : a young man's battle and triumph over
    anorexia / by Gary A. Grahl.
      p. cm.
      ISBN-13: 978-0-9761547-4-7 (softcover: alk. paper)
      ISBN-10: 0-9761547-4-9
      ISBN-13: 978-0-9761547-7-8 (ebook, PDF)
      ISBN-10: 0-9761547-7-3

      1. Grahl, Gary A.—Health. 2. Anorexia nervosa—
    Patients—United States—Biography. 3. Anorexia nervosa
    —Patients—United States—Rehabilitation.   I. Title.

     RC553.A5G73 2007
     616.85'262'0092   2006931881
     QBI07-600021

Questions regarding content of this book should be addressed to:
American Legacy Media, Clearfield, Utah
Visit us at www.americanlegacymedia.com
info@americanlegacymedia.com

Printed in the United States of America

Distributed in North America by Independent Publishers Group (IPG)
(800) 888- 4741 or (312) 337-0747.

1 2 3 4 5 11 10 09 08 07

To Mom and Dad,
the pinnacles of patience and perseverance.

And to my wife and kids,
for their rich love and support.

CONTENTS

Part Two: The New YOU

INTRODUCTION

Although the character names and places and certain details in this book are changed for confidentiality reasons, the people and personalities are real, and the stories that unfold are based on true events. Their impact still lives on in my life to this day. It is my goal that you will find hope and encouragement while reading these pages, for I firmly believe, and discovered first hand, that recovery is very possible for anyone who wages war against an eating disorder. You need not let anyone tell you otherwise.

As you read, please keep in mind that my process of change did not happen as quickly as the book may imply. My hospitalizations spanned a handful of journeys over three hundred days within a five-year period, (not including outpatient work). Old habits die hard, particularly when dealing with an obstinate, thick skull like mine, so it took some time before I wised up and realized that letting go of my eating disorder lifestyle was preferable to holding on to it.

I also found one thing in common between the eating disorder lifestyle and the process of recovering from it: both have strong elements of hard work and routine. It takes just as much will power to train my brain to memorize a Bible verse or a positive affirmation as it does to drag myself out of bed at 3:30 in the morning to exercise my body to the brink of insanity. Likewise, there is a similar amount of routine involved with going to therapy appointments regularly.

Hence, it was quite liberating when I came to the understanding that I am capable of manipulating my motivation for destructive purposes or for health and personal growth. On some days, like the day I suddenly discovered that I am not responsible for other people's feelings, change can be thrilling. Even so, the daily grind of practicing positive changes toward recovery can also be boring and plain, like sitting in a psychiatric hospital day after day, watching the hands of the clock move like snails.

I say all of this for two reasons. First, I encourage everyone struggling with an eating disorder to listen to those professionals and lay people who encourage you to stay the course of recovery. Putting aside familiar, comfortable, unhealthy routines in order to practice those life-altering techniques recommended by your counselor can be downright strange and awkward, but it is certainly necessary for any type of recovery to work. Sitting around hoping that just the right words of inspiration will suddenly fall out of the sky is an illusion. Recovery requires hard work to change irrational thought patterns, to develop innovative techniques for coping with stress, and to build relationships with those who show that they care for you. And it must be done on a regular basis, for years sometimes, before your newly acquired "you" sticks. Be easy on yourself when a technique you're trying doesn't work or when your efforts get terribly frustrating. Time is a necessary ingredient for your process to work.

Second, this book focuses on two specific inpatient experiences, but the incidents that unfold in these pages were taken from a mixture of the others. Much of my experience on Unit 13 was humdrum, tedious, and lackluster, and would be fine reading to put you to sleep at night. So, I hustled up my recovery process for time's sake by combining some of the highlights of all my hospitalizations into two visits. Moreover, if I sat down and wrote about all of the life-changing encounters I had the privilege to undergo during my visits, I'd probably have to write a series similar in length to Harry Potter. However, I do look forward to sharing more with you as time goes on.

Some may notice that my character isn't the most likeable person at times. On the outside, I showed the world a model citizen; on the inside, I was a confused mess—and it shows in how I thought about myself and lived my life. I was scared to reveal to family and peers the real me, the laborious struggle I was enduring, mainly for fear of rejection. During and since my recovery, I've learned that this fear is very common for people with eating disorders. Many times, I despised who I was and agonized over my lack of an identity. Shame influenced me to punish myself via my eating disorder and other self-harming activities. I felt I deserved every biting hunger pang while I starved myself, every aching muscle during my torturous exercise routines, and every disappointed look I earned from my parents, family, and friends throughout those tumultuous five years.

As you read, please keep in mind that this was my own journey through an eating disorder, and it does not constitute or represent every person's struggle. Each person is unique, and just as people experience eating disorders from a variety of perspectives, there are many creative therapies that could enable recovery. Some people grow fastest by expressing their emotions openly. Some people like to try out a new behavior in the same way they would try on a new pare of pants: one leg at a time. Some work on their assertiveness skills with their teacher. Some make efforts to improve their prayer life with God, or find little nuggets of gold in the form of Bible verses that hit home. Some ruminate on positive affirmations from a popular book. Still others focus less on "Me, me, me," and learn to focus on others, which often brings many rewards.

But no matter how a person dresses up professional help—which I strongly believe is mandatory for someone deeply entrenched in an eating disorder—nothing will substitute for hard work and openness to change. A fair amount of swallowing of your stubborn pride doesn't hurt, either. One must put in the challenging hours with counselors, nurses, psychiatrists, social workers, mental health aides, and other caring people who have chosen the study of mental health as their true calling in life. Spend time with these people and those who desire to spend time with you. Step out of your comfort zone and experiment with healthy change, because without it, old patterns of thinking and behaving will remain constant—and so will your eating disorder.

If you are reading this book and struggle with an eating disorder, it is my hope and prayer that you will look deep behind the mask that everyone else sees and accept the grueling struggle for what it is: an eating disorder, not your identity. Accepting your desperate need for help is the first step in recovery—and for some people, the most difficult as well. Professionals can help where well-meaning family and friends cannot. It will be uncomfortable and expensive (both monetarily and emotionally), and will require you to explore a vast, unfamiliar territory. But if you stay with your mission over time, you will be rewarded with the realization that it is possible to change—I did it!

I know this saying has become trite over the years, but it really is true when people say "you aren't alone." You'd be surprised at how many people with the pimple-free faces and perfectly proportioned bodies you envy each day are masters of masks, and looking straight back at you wondering if they can be as "put together" as you are. It is my experience that each of these people would much rather see the real you. Your horrific fear of rejection isn't worth the pain and emotional agony you deal with every day. I hope this book provides you some encouragement to begin your own journey of discovery.

G.G.

Part One: Self Destruction

CHAPTER ONE

SIGN OF THE OBSESSION

I do not like myself. It's that simple. Bloodshot eyes stare back at me in the mirror. Great, I didn't sleep again last night. I gaze at this fat, gelatinous figure with short legs and a long torso. My body reminds me of a squashed Play-Doh figurine. I'm a fifteen-year-old boy, and feel like a pregnant hippo.

That's because you're fat and flabby.

My folks say my stomach and face have a sunken-in look, and harp on me to gain weight. They're "sick and tired" of my "outlandish" exercise routines and "bizarre" dieting rituals. Jogs around the outskirts of our quaint little town when the wind chill reads in at thirty below freezing and dinners consisting of mustard on warm egg whites don't cut it with them anymore.

You're an embarrassment to the entire family.

My real statistics: five feet and eight inches tall, 110 pounds. But it's not skinny enough, not "cut" enough in my muscles, not—

Yeah, yeah—just get to work.

Yes, sir.

I pedal my sore feet like a madman as I approach the end of my ten-mile stationary bike ride. The CNN News blares in front of me, coating the living room with a vaguely blue glow. I love this news. It follows the same pattern every half hour: world news, weather, sports, world news, weather, sports.... It's a routine, something I command my life around.

Dad comes thumping down the steps. "Morning, Gary."

"Morning." *Huff, huff, huff.*

He sits at the living room desk, silently agonizing over this month's bills as usual.

My frantic ride is finally over. Sweat pours from my brow. My T-shirt is drenched. It's time for calisthenics. I pound out push-ups despite my exhaustion. "Sixty-four, sixty-five, sixty-six..."

Dad finishes his tasks and heads upstairs to breakfast. He comes back downstairs fifteen minutes later and goes into our utility room to strap on his boots for work. He finishes and shuts off the light, which cues my next response.

"Bye, Dad. Have a nice—"

The door clicks shut behind him.

He didn't say his usual good-bye.

Without a break in the action, I position my feet under the couch, preparing to whip out my standard three hundred sit-ups. I'm sleepy, physically drained, exasperated, and seriously hungry. I can't wait to sink my teeth into some puffed wheat and skim milk. My mouth begins to water.

You have to earn it first.

I breathe a heavy sigh. Okay, back to work. "One, two, three, four..."

The door slowly cracks open. What the—? Dad comes walking back into the house, weeping like a baby! He makes his way over to me, kneels down, and throws his arms around me in a monstrous bear hug.

Don't stop. Keep pushing onward.

"Gary, I hope you get the help you need on this unit today. Your mother and I just don't know what to do with you anymore. I love you, son. I love you."

I totally ignore my father.

"Fifteen, sixteen, seventeen..."

What are you doing? How selfish can you be?

I feel Dad's tears trickle onto my cheeks and roll down my neck as I increase my pace. I pull my father's big bumblebee body with every repetition. My muscles burn something awful. Dad's embrace progressively squeezes tighter and tighter as my breathing becomes ever more laborious.

This is hard. Get off!

After what seems like an eternity, Dad releases his hold. He pushes himself up, still whimpering, blows his nose with his handkerchief, and shuffles back out the door.

"Two hundred ninety-eight, two hundred ninety-nine, three hundred. Whew!"

I sit up to rest. Guilt squashes me like a bug.

How could you do this to him after all he's done for you? He deserves better than someone like you. He almost became famous and made it to the big leagues, you know.

Yes, I think I'm aware of that fact.

It's your job to make him happy and follow suit. You've got the tools.

Will IT ever go away?

No.

I hate myself. I'm such an idiot.

Amen.

Oh, well. I need to have breakfast before it gets too late. I hope I still have my twenty minutes to eat. My breakfast: Exactly three tablespoons of skim milk over exactly three tablespoons of puffed wheat. Gosh, I'm *starving*. Of course, I would never tell anyone this.

CHAPTER TWO

Helpless

My folks are into subtle hinting. They do this by saying, "Gary Alan Grahl, you look pathetic." I take it as a compliment. That means I'm getting skinnier.

You're such a baby. All a baby does is sleep, poop, eat, and cry, with no expectation to meet his own needs. What a life!

Where does this voice come from?

I've learned that since my family "loves" me, they eventually break down and carry my responsibility. All I need to do is appear boggled over some basic task, and someone will come running to save me. I resent this in myself, but I can't seem to do anything to fix it. Why do I keep this up?

Because you're pathetic, that's why.

One time, I was restringing my baseball catcher's mitt in the living room while Dad sat in his shabby recliner reading the paper. He glanced up from the sports page, noticing my battle with the cowhide. After a minute or two of watching me, he chucked his paper to the floor, came over to me with that I'd-better-help-Gary-because-he-can't-do-it-himself look, and snatched the mitt out of my hand.

Anger surged within me. At first, I wanted to say, "Dad, just leave me alone! I'll do it myself." But instead...

"Here, let me help you with that," said Dad, futzing with my mitt.

I stay quiet.

"There, that's better." He hands it back to me and returns to his chair, shaking his head.

"Thanks, Dad."

A mixture of humiliation and helplessness usually follow close behind in moments like this.

Hey, he's your dad. How can you sit there and allow an opportunity for him to show love fly out the window? He's worked his fingers to the bone for you over the years. On the other hand, you could have said no and—

Well, then, why didn't I say it?

You're not capable. Can't you see that?

CHAPTER THREE

THE RIDE

It's Monday morning. Rain pours down in sheets as I make my way to the car and settle in the passenger seat. The familiar cigarette-smoke film on the windshield emits a disgusting aroma that assaults my nasal passages. Mom involuntarily reaches into her purse. I cough and grudgingly roll down the window when she lights up a smoke. She knows exactly what I'm doing but ignores my act. Subtle hinting must be genetic. Why can't we just talk openly about this?

Talking about feelings is evil, that's why. So just sit there and be quiet.

Our destination is Unit 13, a psychiatric ward at Saint Abernathy Hospital, where I will be admitted as an inpatient, although to me it feels like an inmate. My crime: anorexia nervosa. It sounds like some third-world disease. At least, that's what we thought before a nurse explained it to Mom and me last Friday during a medical assessment. Mom became concerned that something was rotten in Denmark with my weird exercise habits and just happened to catch an advertisement over the radio for the hospital's eating disorders program. So, the next thing I knew, she dragged me in for an evaluation. I politely obeyed, of course. I don't know any other way, no matter how I feel.

I wasn't particular happy about the fact that she took me out of my afternoon chemistry class. We usually received time in class to do our homework. Now I was looking at balancing chemical equations and studying the periodic table at home, which would dig into precious exercise time.

The good news was that the appointment flowed rather quickly.

We met with a nurse named Hadie who had constant sniffles. She took my weight and vitals, then asked me a boat load of questions:

"So, how often do you exercise?" *Sniff.*

Not enough.

"Do you every find yourself getting very upset with your family?" *Sniff.*

I haven't given you permission to be angry.

"Do you look in the mirror and believe you're fat?" *Sniff.*

But you are fat.

"When was the last time you thought about food? *Sniff, sniff.*

When was the last time you didn't?

"Do you ever feel like you must say what you believe others want to hear in order to prevent them from getting upset with you?" *Sniff.*

Of course, duh! It's your job to keep everyone happy.

"Do you ever feel disappointed because you never do things well enough, no matter how hard you try?" *Sniff, sniff.*

Feel disappointed? You are a disappointment.

"Are you ever satisfied with your weight?" *Sniiiiiiff.*

With a little more effort, you really can get to ninety pounds. You'll be much happier at that weight, trust me.

Mom just sat quietly off to the side through most of the interview and barely said a word. Embarrassment and humiliation hid themselves behind her pleasant smile. I learned from the best.

After a brief meeting with other professionals on the unit, the sniffing nurse came back with the sad news: They recommended I go inpatient for my safety.

There's nothing wrong with you, but you better not argue with these people; you might hurt their feelings in some way and wouldn't be able to handle it.

Are you sure? I mean, they are adults and everything and—

Who gave you permission to question me?

Sorry, I just thought—

If you ever want to get to the point of being happy, then I'll do the thinking around here, understand?

Yes, sir.

There was not much discussion once we got home. Shock had set in, which was a great excuse for not talking about anything, particularly feelings—

Watch your mouth, young man! Don't say that word.

Sorry, again.

You say that a lot, don't you?

We immediately began planning for the change in my schedule. There would need to be a proper excuse for school, the issue of homework, my exercise rout—Oh my gosh! My exercise routine!

Now how could you forget about that? You have to start making up time since you're not going to be able to spend your usual five hours a day exercising at this place.

Panic set in hard, and lasted for the rest of the weekend. It spelled more sets of push-ups, a longer run, one hundred fewer calories per meal, and only three hours of sleep last night.

The car ride is long and quiet this morning. I yawn a lot and pretend I'm a prisoner of war going off to a concentration camp. A scene from *Rambo* flashes in front of my mind's eye. I'm Sylvester Stallone being tortured in pig feces. Mom attempts to rationalize her anxiety by giving me a pep talk between puffs on her cigarette. I'm doing fine, however.

"I hope this works for you, Gary. You can't keep doing this to yourself."

"I know."

"You're going to hurt yourself if you keep this up."

"I know."

"Your father and I just don't know what to do with you anymore. Don't you know that we're trying to help you?"

"I know."

"Why don't you stop?"

"I don't know."

I wish I did know how to stop. I hate putting my parents through this misery. They're such great people. They pretty much do everything for me. Maybe that has something to do with it, I don't know. Deep down I have this sense that God didn't intend my life to be like a constant stomach ache, with never-ending worries about how that number will read on the scale, how many calories I've eaten, how fat my stomach feels, or how painful my next workout is going to be. I don't want to worry my parents or cause them any problems because they really are great. I just can't figure out what's wrong with me. I'm not looking to gain the world. I just want to be able to snack on a frozen burrito after school without–

"Gary, answer me."

"Huh? Oh, uh... I don't know."

Go, Coach Mom.

Quiet—that's my mom you're referring to.

So shoot me.

On the other hand, this hospital thing will fit my lifestyle quite nicely since I've recently become allergic to people. Social interaction makes me break out in a terrible rash called guilt; I simply can't seem to please enough people, no matter how hard I try. To remedy this ailment, I've taken to prescribing my own medication; it's called "exercising my tail off in isolation, each time to the extent of my muscles crying out in pain." It works like a charm, and helps me avoid a different sort of pain—rejection by my peers. What would happen if I actually told someone an honest opinion that he didn't like, or disagreed with him, shared my fe—

Excuse me! Didn't I tell you not to use the "f" word again?

Sorry.

Why don't we make that your middle name?

CHAPTER FOUR

AND YOUR NAME IS...?

We drive in a rainstorm down a long, narrow road and reach the remote grounds of Saint Abernathy Hospital. A monstrous brick structure, it's sheltered in a private nook just off the downtown thoroughfare. A speed bump welcomes us by socking our heads into the ceiling. We drive around for a while to find the closest parking spot. After what seems like two days, Mom succumbs to the fact that this hunt is useless, and we end up venturing into the overflow lot. We get out and hurry ourselves toward the entrance to get out of the rain. As we reach the sidewalk, three cars pull out of their parking spots right next to the building.

"Isn't that just par for the course," says Mom.

We approach the admissions desk and state our names. A middle-aged woman with beehive hair and a cup of coffee asks for our insurance card before even saying hello. Her nametag says "Gert." No wonder she's in a grumpy mood. Mom hands the card over while brushing raindrops from her jacket. We wait patiently as this woman's fingers play with the computer keyboard like it's a Steinway and she's a concert pianist.

"Just to double check, that's Unit 13, correct?" asks the receptionist.

Our heads bobble. The receptionist suddenly looks sorry for us, as if Unit 13 is a place for kooks.

It is.

"It's amazing how everything is so computerized and fast nowadays," says Mom.

Good idea, Mom. Change the subject.

We all nod and smile in agreement. It's what Mom and I do best.

After finishing the paperwork to enlist in the Unit 13 ranks, we make our way to the elevator. I'd rather take a detour up the stairs to burn more calories but Mom would question my motive. I'm not up for a sermon right now. On the way to the third floor, Mom reminisces. I listen patiently.

"It seems like only yesterday when I was going down this elevator to take you home. You were such a happy, chubby baby. You were so solid in middle school, too."

She means fat.

"It's too bad you don't have some of that pudginess right now, huh, Gary?" She forces a chuckle.

Yeah, she wants you to stay good and plump so you won't embarrass her when people see you with her. Then she doesn't have to provide all sorts of creative commentary for how you look.

"Yeah," I say, trying even harder to force a chuckle.

The elevator doors open. We're lost already.

"Let's see," says Mom, deep in thought, "where do we go? Maybe we should ask someone."

I look at the directions on the wall, the ones in *large print* and hitting me right in the face. "I think it's this way, Mom."

"Umm...yes, you there," says Mom, cornering a candy striper pushing a bin of laundry. "Could you please tell me where the psychiatric unit is? Silly me, we were just here last week and I can't seem to remember which way to go."

The teenager displays her shiny silver braces and points her finger down the hallway in the same direction I had indicated.

"Oh, I see, thank you." Of course, my mom pays attention to her.

We make our way down a hallway that juts and jitters like a maze. I suddenly feel like a lab rat in some kind of psych experiment. There's a light at the end of the tunnel with people bustling about. Above me, a sign reads "Unit 13—General Psychiatric" loud and strong.

Butterflies dance in my stomach.

So much for being psyched up—no pun intended.

A perky receptionist with frizzy red hair greets us upon arrival. I dub her Wal-Mart because she reminds me of the employees who greet people at the front doors.

"Hello there! Welcome to Unit 13."

I don't know whether to feel welcomed or paranoid. I quickly revert to an incidental question to break though the awkward moment.

"If we're on the third floor, why is this unit called Unit 13?"

"'Because traditionally, we've been the first unit on this wing of the hospital on the third floor," Wal-Mart explains. "Hence, the one before the number three, which put together make '13.' Other units on this floor are labeled '23,' '33,' '43,' and so on."

Gee, they're brilliant here, aren't they.

Wal-Mart turns to Mom, and they exchange pleasantries while I scout out the fort. The nurse's station is positioned at the junction of two hallways that form a ninety-degree angle. Coming up one of the hallways are two inmates: one a stout woman with a long face donning tight-fitting gray sweats, and the other a petite teenage girl wearing baggy sweats and a tight ponytail. They've come to investigate the new guy no doubt. The girl shoots me a quick look. I smile. She continues on without a change in expression. I wonder if I passed inspection.

"It's great to see you folks again. I'll page Greta for you," Wal-Mart says, reaching for the phone.

Mom has this deer-in-the-headlights expression. I'm scared for her. Will she be able to handle all of this? I worry about her. She's been stressed lately.

It's your job to keep her happy.

I'm not doing so hot, am I?

Keep trying. Her feelings are your responsibility.

Yes, sir. I'll keep trying, sir.

Greta McTavish, director of inpatient services on Unit 13, heartily greets us at the desk. Confidence oozes from her every pore. She grips our hands in a firm shake. After a quick check of my bulging suitcase—they confiscate the two ten-pound dumbbells—she blazes a trail to the examination room. After all of us enter, Greta notices we're one chair short. She turns back to the door to hunt down another one.

Stand.

"That's okay," I say. "I'll stand,"

"Nonsense, there's a chair in the room next door. I'll go get it."

You must stand.

"No, really. I'll stand. I've been sitting all morning anyhow."

"Gaa-ry!" cries Mom. "You just don't like to sit because it hurts your skinny little rump. There's no meat on your bones."

Standing burns more calories, but we'll keep that our little secret, okay?

I step to the side, though still blocking part of Greta's path. She throws me a knowing grin. Can she read my mind? I answer back with a smile.

"Gary, I'll get that chair for you," says Greta.

She bounds out the door, brushing my shoulder as she passes. Moments later, she returns with a wooden chair. I never had a chance, did I?

She may have won the battle but we'll win the war.

CHAPTER FIVE

THE IRON GIANT

The conversation starts out like most, superficial and dull. It's a game I don't care to play, although I'm quite good at it. Greta begins by commenting on the weather. Mom reciprocates. There's a shallow attempt at humor from Greta, which fails but manages to extract some kind of fake chuckle from Mom and me. Then, the main course of questions is tossed on a plate in front of me.

"So, Gary," says Greta, getting comfortable in the chair. "How are you doing today?"

"Good."

"Are you ready for the long road ahead of you?"

I shrug my shoulders and smile. I always smile in front of others. I smile when I'm happy. I smile when I'm sad. I smile when I'm upset. I smile when I'm embarrassed. Heck, I'd probably smile if an elephant was crushing my foot right now, all for...for...I don't know why. All I know is that I'm terrified of allowing anyone so much as a glimmer of the authentic me, whoever that is. At least smiles are safe.

"Gaa-ry!" says Mom. "Why don't you talk to Greta? This is the time to get help."

Help? Who needs help? You're doing just fine.

"I don't know what to say."

"Anything, talk about anything. Just talk. Lots of things are fair game," Mom pushes. "What about that one time you told me about being teased?"

Remember, back in elementary school, when he took great pleasure in squashing your—

Keep that jerk out of this, will you?

This silly mother issue isn't going to go disappear, you know.

I said shut up!

You're right. Talking will only cause more hurt feelings. I've trained you well.

Guilt thrusts its sword into my side. My throat suddenly forgets how to talk. I heave a heavy sigh. Mom's is heavier, and includes a shaking head.

Greta gets wise in a hurry to the fact that she's not going to get anywhere with me right now. Greta and Mom head out the door for a brief powwow. My senses get a wake-up call from a washed-out gown that slaps me in the chest and falls to the examination table.

"Whoops!" says Greta, innocently. "Sorry, Gary, I thought you were looking. I'd like for you to change into this and knock when you're ready. I'll get your vitals and weight, and then we'll take a quick tour of the unit."

As soon as the door shuts, I immediately strip to my underwear and look into the full-length mirror on the wall. It's a familiar picture I gawk at dozens of times daily. I reach my arms high into the air as if I'm signaling a touchdown. I can feel my skin stretch tautly over twelve protruding ribs like thin plastic on a freezer-wrapped chicken. I turn to the side and bend over. The vertebrae on my backbone stick out sharply. The lower part of my spine is calloused black and blue from months of doing endless sit-ups on our linoleum bathroom floor. Pride momentarily rips through my conscience.

But, it's just not good enough. You're still so flabby and soft. Your muscles aren't cut enough. Your legs aren't long enough. You're nothing but a cow.

Next to the mirror sits one of the most intimidating pieces of equipment ever invented by man: the scale. It's a tall steel monster with a heavy iron block that slides across a steel ruler, like the one the wrestlers use at school. Do I dare look this morning?

Of course. Your day will be unbearable if you don't.

I find my body automatically stepping up onto the cool metal platform, shifting the black block across the ruler to find—Aw man, what a rip! Is this thing broken? I do *not* weight this much.

A knock comes at the door.

"Gary? Are you ready?"

I quickly hop off the scale, put my hospital gown back on, and sit up straight on the exam table. "Yeah."

Greta and mom come back in. A stethoscope hangs around Greta's neck, and she's carrying a clipboard. I feel uncomfortable. Greta takes my blood pressure, pulse, height, and weight. It's pathetic to her, a badge of courage to me: pulse, thirty-five beats per minute; height, five feet, eight inches; weight, 109 pounds—down a whole pound from yesterday. I shake my head like I'm really disappointed so Greta and Mom don't think I'm satisfied about the low weight.

Atta boy.

"Wow," says Greta, making notes on what I assume is my chart. "You are a sick young man. Given your activity level, your medium-to-large bone structure, and the fact that you're a growing teenage boy, you should be weighing in the neighborhood of 155 pounds, minimum."

She gives her head a little shake while ripping off the Velcro blood pressure cuff.

She steps out of the room so I can change into my civilian clothes, then returns with my mother.

"I know we briefly touched on this last Friday during your initial evaluation," says Greta, "but take me again through a typical day for you."

Here's my chance to impress her once again.

"Well, I get up at 3:30 every morning—"

"In the morning?" cries Mom. "*Gaa*-ry! Why do you have to get up so early?"

"To exercise. I'm usually up anyhow."

Actually, I'm dead tired at that hour, but I've been forcing myself to rise earlier for months in order to accommodate my increased workout load.

"What do you do from there?" asks Greta.

"Well, I come downstairs and turn on the CNN News. After warm-up stretching I head outside for twenty fifty-yard sprints. Then it's back inside for fifteen miles on the exercise bike under heavy tension, five hundred sit-ups, three hundred push-ups, one hundred swings of my baseball bat both left and right handed, three hundred jumping jacks, and one hundred karate kicks with my right and left legs," I say, enthusiasm beginning to spill over in my tone. Thinking about my exercise routine gets my adrenaline surging. "Sometimes in the winter when the snow is really high, I like to add a three-mile run in our back field." I don't mention that I do this wearing heavy snow boots because I have to kick higher that way. "Finally, it's my cool down stretching for about five minutes. Then it's off to breakfast."

"Ha! He barely eats enough to keep a bird alive," Mom mutters.

"How long have you kept this routine going?" asks Greta.

"About a year now."

Mom's hand frantically dives for her purse, then suddenly stops short as she realizes she can't light up in the hospital.

"Continue," says Greta.

"Breakfast is usually three tablespoons of cereal with three tablespoons of skim milk. Then it's—"

"Ha!" exclaims Mom, her voice wheezy and heavy even though she's still working hard to maintain a pleasant smile. "It takes him nearly half an hour to eat that, too!"

I keep smiling, pretending that I'm not feeling perturbed about being interrupted.

"Then it's off to school. Lunch is usually a half peanut butter and jelly sandwich, an apple, and some skim milk. Sometimes, I eat just the apple. After school I come home and do another hour and a half of exercising, usually weight lifting and more bat swinging. For dinner I have some type of meat, potato product, and a vegetable—no more than three hundred to five hundred calories, depending on how much I exercised," I say, trying to be as thorough as possible. I'm secretly hoping to elicit some raised eyebrows and wide eyes. "Then it's off to do my homework or watch some TV, do my five-mile run, and hit the hay. A lot of nights, I like swinging my bat in my room before bed while I listen to some music."

"He broke his brother's stereo while swinging that thing," Mom interjects. Her smile is looking more and more forced. "And what about the time you took out your bedroom window, Gary?"

Actually, I forgot about that.

"Oh, and then there's his habit of walking around our pool table after meals. He thinks we don't know what he's doing, but we do."

The CIA would be impressed.

Greta repositions in her chair, focusing on me. "Tell me again, why do you do so much exercising?"

"I'm in training to be a professional baseball player."

Mom is getting more steamed by the minute. Her lips are pursed together like she slurped some bad coffee. I have never seen her quite this agitated. The attention feels uncomfortable, but also good for some reason.

Why do you put your loving mother through this headache? You're embarrassing her.

"*Gaa*-ry! How the heck do you expect to play baseball with your weight so low? How do you know you're going to even wake up the next—"

"Pardon me for interrupting, Mrs. Grahl—"

Thank you. Someone put this poor woman on ice.

"—but I don't think it's going to do any good raising our voices in speculation right now," Greta says. "I do like that you're expressing your feelings. I think it helps Gary understand how much this affects you. However, I think it's important to use 'I' messages, like 'I'm feeling angry' or 'I don't like how your lifestyle is tearing you down.' We are responsible for our own feelings and actions."

Huh?

Mom and I look at each other, dumbfounded. That's not how we work.

I've trained you well.

I yawn. Another early wake-up call this morning with an intense workout has pacified my body. My eyelids feel like anchors.

Greta gets to the point. "Gary, you're emaciated, but you see someone who's fat; you say you're training for baseball, but your exercise patterns are tearing your body apart; you're ravenously hungry, but deceive yourself into thinking your stomach is full—"

Wait a minute, how does she know that I—

"—You cannot be satisfied unless your muscles are crying out in pain and soreness; you will not allow yourself to enjoy the simple pleasures of life, but instead feel shame and guilt if success comes your way; you feel like you don't deserve good things in life—"

For a brief moment, Greta pokes her head through the window of my private world, causing me to duck and hide.

You will not listen to this hogwash! How dare this stranger tell you who she thinks you are?

Anger swells in my throat. What is that?

Authorized personnel only!

Fear pinches my nerves. What's going on here? Maybe I'm not such a unique situation. Maybe I'm not so special after all. Maybe there is something wrong with—

You are the toughest kid in the world. No one can outdo you in exercise, self-discipline, sheer will power, and losing weight. You are a Special Forces kid, the Green Beret and Navy SEAL of your time. Take pride in how special you are.

I stare blankly at the wall over Greta's shoulder. My mind is empty.

You are the best, aren't you?

Well, I...I...guess so. My mouth lets out another lion's roar yawn. Wow, I'm tired. I want a bed.

"Gary? Gary?" says Greta. "Are you okay? You look a little dazed all of a sudden."

"Huh? Oh—uh, I'm okay. I'm just a little tired, that's all."

I smile, smile, and smile some more, then yawn again. I wonder what meals are like up here. I won't be doing much walking this morning.

Lunch will be two bites.

I usually only have just an apple on Mondays. I wonder if I can get something like that for lunch. Come to think of it, I won't be doing the same exercise routine for the rest of the day.

Skip supper.

I suddenly become aware of a silence in the room. Greta and Mom look intently at me. Greta is grinning. Mom is scowling behind her smile.

"*Gaa*-ry!" says Mom, looking furious that I'm not paying attention. "Are you even hearing a word we're saying?"

Just nod and smile, Gary, just nod and smile.

I nod, feeling incredibly guilty.

CHAPTER SIX

THE FIFTY-CENT TOUR

The tour is rather brief. Unit 13 reminds me of the nursing home I visited my grandma in a few years ago. There's a dining room, game room with a Ping–Pong and pool table, a large multipurpose room, and—I do a double take—a smoking room.

We come to a sterile, secluded room that's housed behind a door reinforced with layers of thick steel. There's nothing inside except a cot. The cold concrete floor and padded walls are gleaming white.

"What's this room?" I ask.

"It's called the Quiet Room. We reserve it for patients that are not deemed, how shall I say, appropriate to be out and about with other patients. We use it only in extreme cases, for those who might be of harm to self or others. Shall we move on?" Greta says in a voice that lets me know it's not a question.

Across from the dining room hangs a gigantic dry-erase board with the day's schedule. It reads like this:

8:15 Breakfast

9:15 Exercise Class

10:30 Group Therapy

12:00 Lunch

1:00   Stress Management

2:30   Occupational Therapy

5:30   Dinner

9:30   Reflections

11:00 Lights Out

Only three hours and forty-five minutes between breakfast and lunch? My breakfast is still digesting. We get only an hour for lunch? What is Occupational Therapy? Occupation means work—will I have a part-time job or something? No exercise in the afternoon? I'll feel like a blimp by dinner.

The stop I've anticipated for the last hour comes into view: the exercise room. Two rickety stationary bikes sit in the corner (the chain is off one of them), a punching bag hangs from the ceiling, and a shabby rowing machine that desperately needs to be power washed sits all by its lonesome on the floor by the door.

I'm extremely disappointed.

"Welcome to our gym," says Greta, giving the punching bag a good swat. "We have these exercise videos that we follow each morning, just enough to give patients some healthy movement during their busy days. Although, I'm not sure your doctor has ordered exercise class for you quite yet." I'm sorry, but I think my ears got sucked inside out. I thought I heard you say no exercise class has been ordered for me. You're not kidding, are you? It's not funny to joke about something like this to a guy like me.

Panic sets in, but I hold fast to my calm and collected position. "Oh?"

Who is this doctor of yours and what business does he have butting into your life?

"Dr. Buckmier will be your psychiatrist. He will meet with you every morning for therapy and monitor any medication you might need to be on. He's an early bird, so he generally tries to grab people before breakfast."

What the—therapy? Medication? He grabs people?

"How come he won't let me do exercise class?" Asking questions is not my cup of coffee, but when it comes to a stranger messing around with my exercise routine, everything else takes second place.

"For patients with anorexia, he generally likes to gather blood work, monitor body weight, and get a therapy session or two under his belt before he allows exercise. How do you feel about this?"

Keep wearing your smile. Feeling anything else is unbearable for you.

"That's understandable," I say, smiling widely. My demeanor meter reads "cooperative and in control at all times." To me, sincere emotional expression in public is like purposely walking into a colony of killer bees and smashing the hive—it's my fault that I'll get stung from all sides, and it's going to hurt.

So, this doctor wants to battle, huh? Well, if he's shopping for a good battle he came to the right supermarket.

CHAPTER SEVEN

CHANDRA

M y room is awesome. Two beds sit side by side equipped with more gadgetry than Air Force One. I pull open the curtains of a monstrous window to take a gander at a view that overlooks the hospital courtyard. Three hospital personnel dressed in white sit at a picnic table, puffing away on cigarettes. In the background I see a large, medieval-type building with "Sisters of Saint Abernathy" inscribed at the top. An enormous Green Bay Packers flag flaps in the breeze next to a massive stone statue of someone I don't recognize but who is obviously important. The only complaint I have about the accommodations is that the room's stationed only a good spit away from the nurse's desk.

You'll need to exhibit the utmost in stealth while executing workouts.

"So far, you will have your own pad until patient numbers increase. There are only ten patients on the unit right now, so we'll keep you posted." Greta glances at her watch and looks up again, still smiling of course. "Well, I need to scoot for now. It was nice seeing you again, Mrs. Grahl. Gary, your nurse will be in shortly to introduce herself. We'll meet up again sometime soon." She exits the room, leaving me alone with Mom and a suitcase.

"Boy, this is quite a room," says Mom. I was so wrapped up with figuring out a covert exercise plan that I almost forgot she was there. We huddle for safety under the umbrella of small talk while Mom stuffs socks in a drawer.

"Well, I best be going for now. Dad and I will be up tomorrow to see how you're doing. If you need anything, just give us a call." She hesitates.

Are those watery eyes I see? Oh, man, this is uncomfortable. Do we hug now or what? Actually, I'd like to try but—

Are you crazy? Don't give her a hug. It will feel indescribably awkward. You won't be able to handle it.

Mom moves in closer to me, eyes still gazing around the room. She reaches up her arm and—

Oh, no, here it comes. This is going to feel weird.

—gently rests fingertips on my forearm, jerking them away quickly, as if my skin burns her.

"You get better now Gary, you hear? You've got a lot of people rooting for you."

"Okay, Mom."

She turns and scurries out the door. I stand by myself, the way I like it. An adventure land of unique proportions is set before me. I am alone. Or am I?

I barely have time to finish unpacking when there's a knock at the door. A tall, lanky, swarthy-looking woman of what I will guess is Jamaican decent swaggers into the room. She packs two freshly-sharpened pencils and some computer-generated, fill-in-the-circle, multiple-choice format something or other.

"Knock, knock. Is anyone home?" *Sniff.* "Gary? My name is Hadie. I met you and your mom when you came in last week?" *Sniff.* "I'll be your nurse for this morning. You'll have a different main nurse each shift." *Sniff.* "It's nice to see you again." *Sniff.*

"'Yeah, nice to see you." I reach out for her hand. It feels like I'm grasping a warm-blooded skeleton. Wrinkles cover her light complexion. Her eyes are magnified by the thick, bug-eyed glasses that make her pupils balloon to the size of bowling balls.

"I hope you're getting adjusted okay," says Hadie. "How are you feeling?" *Sniff.*

Like she really cares?

"Fine, thanks."

"If there's anything you need, just let me know. What do you think of the place?" *Sniff.*

"It's nice."

For a prison.

"Well, you're in good hands up here." *Sniff.* "Your doctor has ordered for you to fill out this personality inventory." *Sniff.* "It will aid us in designing your treatment protocol." *Sniff.* "It will take you approximately three hours—"

Three hours? Ancient civilizations have been built and conquered in shorter periods of time, for crying out loud.

"—but you do not need to complete it in one sitting. However," *sniff,* "Dr. Buckmier does wish for you to finish before you turn in for the evening." *Sniiiiiiiiiff.* "Do you have any questions?"

"Uh..."

"Very well then. Group therapy will be in thirty minutes." *Sniff.* "I hope you find support and encouragement up here. My many years of experience as a nurse on this unit have shown me that the more a patient shares with others, the faster the person learns, grows, and heals." *Sniff.* "It's like the old saying goes—"

Group therapy?

Never mind that. Think about what's for lunch.

"—when times get tough, talking tops walking, ha, ha, ha." *Sniff.* "I remember one time when—"

You should have pedaled ten more minutes on the bike this morning. That walking around the pool table wasn't nearly as strenuous as pumping bike pedals—

Shh! I'm trying to listen.

You could have burned at least 120 more calories. You should have—

I said shh!

Don't shush me.

"—and so by doing that," *sniff,* "you should be just fine. Do you have anymore questions?"

Not wanting to put another quarter in Hadie's jukebox, I shake my head.

"Well, I'll leave you alone to finish unpacking." *Sniff, sniff.* "The inventory is on the table. I'll check in with you at lunch." *Sniff.* "Bye." *Sniiiiiiiiiiff.* Out the door she goes.

I finish finding a home for my toiletries and the rest of my clothes and sit down to take a quick peek at the personality inventory. I flip to the back. It contains 478 questions. I sigh. I scan the pages, previewing the contents, take a deep breath, and get to work.

I get through question 150 and stop.

You should be running in place right now. What's wrong with you?

I grunt in frustration.

I'm serious. Get off your butt and move.

I don't want to.

You must. You have no choice, remember? I'm in charge.

Taking my mind off of, well, what ever IT is, leads me to engage in one of my favorite hobbies: talking to myself. I remind myself that experts say it's actually quite healthy and natural.

"Let's see, the next question: 'Do you feel intimidated in a group of strange people?' Hmmm..."

A voice from the doorway startles me. "I guess that depends on who's in the group."

A tingling jolts down my spine as if I had just touched an electric fence. The cute girl from earlier this morning leans against the doorframe with her arms folded.

Make sure you don't spoil her day with your grumpiness.

My face instantly changes to a look of pleasant surprise, like I just saw my birthday cake with candles blazing.

"Oh, uh, hi," I say, clearing my throat.

"I thought those questions were, like, really stupid. What do they think we are, experimental monkeys or something? It's, like, the weirdest test I've ever taken. I'm Chandra, and you are...?"

"Gary."

"So you're the new guy around here. Are you coming to group therapy?

"I think so."

You don't even know what that is, but good cover-up.

"Well, they made me go right away. I tried to skip it once and hid out in the exercise room doing my homework. Atalanta came down and threatened to take away my weekend pass. I wasn't going to miss that, so I slammed my books down and went to group. Have you met her yet?"

My mind doesn't want to register anything at the moment. I'm too engrossed in how pretty she is. "I'm sorry, who?"

"Atalanta, the nurse, you silly..." she wanders over to the small desk where I'm sitting to peek at what I'm doing. "She's a piece of work. I looked up the meaning of her name one time in one of those baby name books. It means, like, 'mean adversary' or something. Go figure."

She's leaning over my shoulder when she straightens suddenly. "Uh, oh!" says Chandra. "Speak of the devil. Like, here she comes."

A low, gravely voice materializes from out in the corridor. "Group therapy! Group therapy! Come on you two. Get your royal bahunkas down to the group room. Let's go. Move it! Move it!"

"See what I mean?" says Chandra out of the side of her mouth.

"Okay, be right there." I smile and try to look enthusiastic and excited.

What a fake. What a waste.

CHAPTER EIGHT

GROUP THERAPY

Ten of us sit in a circle facing one another. Spirals of fine vapor rise from Styrofoam cups of hot coffee clasped in many a hand. This is the heart of treatment, the thump-thump of psychological warfare, the fix-it shop of emotional wrecks. This is group therapy.

Arty is our fearless leader, a social worker and director of therapeutic groups on Unit 13. He's shaped like a pear. His very-black facial hair is carefully manicured to the same perfection that Dad has me cut our front lawn. His eyes are Caribbean blue and are riveted on whoever gets trapped in his line of vision. There's something intimidating about him, but I can't seem to put my finger on it yet. A nurse with "Doreen" on her nametag, apparently his faithful sidekick, sits opposite Arty. The last patient enters the room and shuts the door. Small talk comes to a hush. Let's play ball.

"Well, good morning, everyone. Most of you know me, but for the new folks, I'm Arty, a social worker on the unit. Welcome to group therapy. We've got plenty on our plate today so let's get started." I wait for him to clap like a kindergarten teacher to get us started, but he just keeps going. "It's routine for me to remind you about confidentiality. Whatever we talk about in here stays in here. We will go around the circle, introduce ourselves, say why we're here, and what we'd like to get from group today. We are each responsible for our own welfare so you may say or not say whatever you'd like. Keep in mind that the more you contribute to group, the more you will grow. With that, let's begin. Would anyone like to get us cooking?"

Arty's eyes meet those of the stocky middle-aged gentleman positioned next to him who, I would guess, weighs in the neighborhood of three hundred pounds. His height might be a pork rind shy of five-foot-nine. He looks like he just saw a ghost.

"My name is Leonard and I am an alcoholic. I also suffer from depression, obesity, high blood pressure, have a history of stroke in my family, and I'm diabetic. This is day seven for me on the unit after being transferred from the Juniper House, a halfway house for alcoholics. It's been pure hell for me now since—"

"Excuse me, Leonard," Arty interrupts. "We'll wait for everyone else to get a chance before going into any significant depth. What would you like to get out of group today?"

"Well, I'd like to get some understanding, some unconditional love, some sort of respect for my condition. Many of you are probably thinking 'Why don't we just shoot this horse and put him out of his misery?' You see, I've been feeling this way—"

Nurse Doreen pipes in. "Ahh, Leonard, remember..."

"I'm sorry, forgive me everyone," says Leonard, blowing his nose on a handkerchief and sticking it back into the front pocket of his flannel shirt.

Now that's gross.

The cycle continues. Various types of patients abound in this crop. Fran was left at home with two young children after her husband fled the state while having an affair with the family's babysitter. Tom is an alcoholic. Bill has depression. Jan has schizophrenia and hears voices. (I can identify with that, although mine isn't an actual voice. At least I don't think it is.) Stan lost his modest farm to bankruptcy after it had been in his family for four generations. Nancy overdosed on aspirin.

Chandra is set to go next. She sits two people to my right, next to her roommate, Mary, who has clinical depression. I'm anxious to hear what she's here for. Guessing from her body size, my money is on an eating disorder.

You won't be able to handle it once the baton is passed to you.

Where's my hole to crawl into?

"I'm Chandra, and I have anorexia and bulimia."

A tinge of jealous rips through my veins, as if I want to be the only one with any eating disorder.

She's thinner than you, too. We'll just have to do something about that, now won't we?

"I've been here two weeks," continues Chandra. "I guess what I want out of group is to get to know others for once."

She gives a little scowl at Arty and then around the room. She spouts a resentful tone and speaks her mind. Something tells me she's been picked on in group lately. I wish I had the guts to talk like that.

My turn arrives. Oh, boy, here we go.

Say something safe.

"My name is Gary and this is my first day. What I'd like to get out of group is to get to know everyone better."

Hey, that actually wasn't so bad. Okay, who's next?

"And why are you here?" asks Arty, not letting me off the hook so easily.

Adrenaline buzzes down my spine.

"I, uh, have, uh—"

Don't say it. You'll feel squeamish.

"—anorexia."

Yuck! That felt so weird coming out of my mouth.

Told you so.

I scan the group and take a quick facial expression inventory. No crinkled noses. No startled stares. No mouths hanging open.

The floor is left wide open. Silence stirs for a moment. It's painful. My eyes find Arty's argyle socks, and I stare at them to avoid meeting anyone's gaze. Leonard can't stand it anymore and breaks. He begins uncoiling his blanket of anxiety. Group veterans groan. He chatters for nearly five minutes straight about the halfway house that just accepted his social worker's recommendation to continue treatment for alcoholism at their facility, which is just down the road from here so he can be close to his wife and sons so they can help him organize the mess of medication his three different doctors have him on but he'd normally have only one physician but since his insurance only covers certain treatment options only with a second opinion, he has to go at his treatment down this route in order for him to remain stable because it would be awful for him to backslide at this point due to the fact that he doesn't know what he would do if the halfway house doesn't take him now that his wife has virtually given up on his situation—

Arty grants patience for a while but then cuts Leonard's cord. The stage opens once again for other lamenters. There are no takers. Leonard pants like a thirsty puppy. He stares at Arty with hope in his eye, begging for one last shot. Arty fires him a quick smile but shakes his head, then hones in on Nancy, Ms. Suicidal. He mercilessly probes her for the remainder of the time in group. All the while she whimpers, ripping tissue after tissue from the box handed to her by Leonard. Arty skillfully extracts emotional pus from her psyche like a skilled dermatologist squeezing a bulging white pimple. This is not pretty. I'm thanking the good Lord I'm not that poor woman right now. After fifteen minutes, she takes a deep breath and admits relief.

Relief? How is that so? He just took her for an emotional roller coaster ride, in front of total strangers no less. Will there be a sequel?

Then it occurs to me: These are not total strangers. There's some kind of common bond going on here, empathy to the max. There's no raising eyebrows, no murmuring behind backs, no laughing or pompous giggling at each other's problems. I wonder what would happen if I—

Don't even think of it. You'd never survive.

"You did well, Nancy," Arty says, "how do you feel?"

"Much better, thanks." She drops one more crumpled tissue on the pile beneath her chair. "It feels good to get that off my chest."

You rock, Nancy.

Our time is almost up. I wonder what's for lunch. I'm actually hungry.

Lunch will be sparse pickings. You've been sitting all morning.

I wish I didn't have to listen to you. I wish I could be like my younger brother, Rick, and eat anything I want without feeling guilty. My mom told me one time that our family can eat anything we want and not gain weight, something about having "the genes." I just want my jeans to fit loosely, that's all.

A tight waistband equals weakness and failure.

I sigh.

"How are you doing over there, Gary?" Arty asks, catching me off guard.

"Hmmm?"

"How're you doing? You've been rather quiet."

I suddenly come to the realization that I'm the only one in group who hasn't said anything beyond the mandatory introduction. That's usually the way things go for me in any group. I stay to the wayside and keep my own little fire burning, praying that nobody notices the flames.

Protect. Stay safe.

"Uh, well...I'm just trying to take everything in. I like to listen."

Arty peers at me suspiciously. I feel my cheeks turning red. I must look like a large beet. The group turns its attention toward me, as if I've said the wrong thing. They await Arty's next move without stirring.

Why is it so quiet in here? Somebody say something.

Arty stares at me, not moving a muscle. My attention reverts once again to his feet, as I determinedly avoid his gaze. If I meet his eyes, it could mean an awful fate, just like seeing the terribly let-down faces I get from Mom and Dad.

Stay away.

I'm trying, I'm trying.

"Well," says Arty, "I guess it's time to close up shop for today."

Whew! That was close. I'm already dreading tomorrow's group. He might bookmark this moment.

CHAPTER NINE

ATALANTA THE PRIVATE INVESTIGATOR

Greta totes a pile of books dealing with anorexia into my room and drops them in my lap before lunch. I like her. There's just something about how she conducts herself around others. She's so genuine, real, and confident. She knows who she is and isn't afraid to show it.

I wish I could get to that level.

I begin scanning through the books and see a reflection of myself on every page. It hits me smack between the eyes. I really do have anorexia. You mean I'm not unique? Lots of other people struggle with this?

Maybe you're a girl.

Shut up.

It says here that even guys get it, though it's rare.

A brown cart rattling down the corridor interrupts me. It brings us food. A man who reminds me of Igor from *Frankenstein* pushes the trolley. We gather around like cows in front of a feeding trough. It's like what happens when Dad tosses freshly snipped grass clipping into the neighbor's pasture. Livestock come galloping from all directions. "It's dessert to them," Dad would always say.

Gosh, it smells good.

You may not eat at will. You didn't earn the calories.

A tray is handed to me. I march directly for the back of the dining room next to a collection of rubber tree plants, far away from the troop. I want to eat alone. If Chandra wants to sit next to me, I'll make an exception.

Stan, the bankrupt farmer, wanders aimlessly through the room with his tray.

Don't look my way. Look over there, look over there, look over there...

He spots the vacancy at my table and hobbles over.

Darn it.

I lift my entrée cover and—Wow! A heaping pile of macaroni and cheese seeps over the side of my plate and spills over onto the tray. Sweet potatoes and corn garnish the rest of the platter. There's chicken noodle soup, rainbow Jell-O, and banana cream pie surrounding my main dish. Whole milk and coffee are my beverages. My stomach growls. It wants to be fed.

It's at this time that my built-in calorie counter automatically shifts into high gear, now an involuntary reaction from a year of strict training. I've virtually memorized the Food Calorie Guide, carrying it with me just about everywhere, including church on occasion.

Fifty...150...275...400...590...640... There's about 1,000 calories on this tray!

I'd love to eat this. It looks so good. It smells heavenly. I'm so hungry.

Stan digs in with two forks. "I bet you're as hungry as I am."

My stomach growls again.

"Not really."

IT has become an all-consuming beast, a thorn in my side, a sickness to overcome and flush out of my system. Yet, I defend IT with stark determination. Why? I have no idea. I don't know if I want to know. I have my reasons, even though I can't figure them out right now.

I yearn to swallow large bites. Instead, I settle for pecking and nibbling like a rooster after spare feed.

Steady now. Eat too much and break the law. You'll suffer the consequences.

Oh, yeah that stupid law.

Unfortunately, I have a law: Though shalt not ingest calories to the point that thou shall feel satisfied. Thou shalt remain hungry. A recent amendment to the law: Thou shalt not eat more than anyone else at thy table, including children. Serious penalties are inflicted for breaking the law: unrelenting guilt that lasts for hours and sometimes days, loss of concentration, mental whippings, increased anxiety, elimination of further meals for the day, and merciless pain in my workouts. Meals must be earned.

Atalanta sits at a table between Chandra and me. Her head twists back and forth as if she's viewing a tennis match. She's sharp as a tack, built like a tank, and quick to catch any clandestine attempt at foolery. Her piercing glare speaks loads: "I've got my eye on you two. Any funny business and I'll have to cut off your thumbs."

This one will be a challenge.

I decide it's time to hang it up for the meal. I'm beginning to lose hungriness, and I can't break my law.

"Is that all you're going to eat?" asks Atalanta. "You hardly touched your plate. What a waste of perfectly good food. Why don't you try and eat a bit more."

I smile and look down.

"Come on, young man. Eat."

I sit defenseless, like a scared little bunny in sight of an owl.

Here, since you can't do anything yourself, let me help you. When she looks away, put your foodless fork in your mouth as if taking a bite.

I follow orders, doing it again, then again. Timing is the key. In between looks, I shuffle food under my plate. My nerves act up at the possibility of being found out.

That should do the trick. It's time to go. You've eaten enough.

I push my chair away from the table and get up. Atalanta just stares at me. She senses that something is up, but can't prove it. I can feel her eyes following me all the way to the cart as I dispose of the evidence.

Whew.

Brush your teeth, then pace the unit. You have at least 200 calories to burn.

Yes, sir.

I wander in and out of each room, scanning bookshelves, pretending to investigate what's outside each window, and, when no one's in view, hit the floor for a dozen push-ups. With twenty minutes of movement completed, I head down to the lounge and plop into a chair next to Chandra.

"How's it going?" says Chandra.

"Good."

"I wish I could walk around like that."

You've been watching?

"Why can't you?"

"They say it's, like, unit protocol for those with eating disorders. I'm surprised they didn't yell at you."

My anxiety hits the fan.

This news changes everything. Get back up and move.

But I'd rather stay put and get to know Chandra better.

You know what you should do.

I hate this. I really want to stay and flirt, but—

You should follow orders, mister!

A minute later, I've covered two rooms.

Maybe I can spend some "active moments" in the exercise room. But that's clear down at the other end of the unit. I'll have to make it past the nurse's station first. They don't want patients alone in their rooms during the day. I approach the desk with caution. Wal-Mart is looking down. Atalanta is busy fingering a freshly baked batch of crabapple muffins. She's been casually firing dubious looks in my direction for the last few minutes, questioning a possible shady scheme on my part. I think the bloodhound in her knows something is up.

"Ah, excuse me, Gary," says Atalanta, wiping crumbs from her lips. "Where do you think you're going?"

Lie.

But lying isn't right.

You will obey me, or else.

"I—uh... I'm looking for my gold necklace my mother gave me for Christmas last year. I think it might have fallen off somewhere down this hall."

"I'll see if anyone has turned it in to the lost and found. Wait here."

Wal-Mart looks up dreamily into the air. "You know, I lost a bracelet my grandmother gave me one time. I ended up digging it out of a bag of flour one day, ha, ha, ha. My grandmother... such a sweet old woman. I remember one time ..."

Much to my relief, Atalanta returns sooner than later, empty handed.

"Nope, nothing back there. I'll alert housekeeping to keep an eye out for it. In the mean time, why don't you go and have a seat. You've burned enough rubber off those shoes for one day."

You are not allowed to sit yet. More calories need to be singed.

But—

Move it! You know better than to disobey an order.

Auugh!

I resort to plan B: the bathroom—my second gym. I put the toilet seat down as if to sit on the throne, but instead hit the floor for fifty push-ups. Thirty seconds later, it is one full minute of running in place with ultra-high leg kicks and a dozen or so rapid trunk twists in between. I turn on the faucet as if to wash my hands, drowning out my heavy breathing of fifty flash-quick jumping jacks. I turn off the water and do deep breathing exercises to calm my pulse and reduce the flush-red coloring in my face. Exactly three minutes later, I open the bathroom door and head toward the drinking fountain to get a drink, mainly for the purpose of expending more time to cool my jets.

Good, no one noticed. Now to—Aaaaah!

"Mr. Grahl?" cries Atalanta, standing directly behind me. "May I have a word with you?"

How did you get there so fast?

Remain calm. You shall not give in.

I follow Atalanta to a private corner near the front desk, feeling embarrassed but careful not to appear too sheepish. Wal-Mart glances over us, grinning.

"You know," starts Atalanta, "I couldn't help but notice you were in the bathroom for a good three minutes. Your face also looks a bit flushed. Are you feeling okay?"

Think quickly, quickly, quickly!

Panic covers my face—my real face, the one behind the mask of pearly teeth I shine in front of Atalanta.

You will not relinquish my command. Lie again.

No, please. God doesn't like it. It's wrong. I hate it.

Then suffer.

"I, uh... "

You must protect me!

"I had to go number two. Then I tried to pop a few acne bombs on my face. I washed when I was done." Practice and skill has gotten me to the point where my face doesn't even turn red this time.

There, that wasn't so bad, was it? You're quite good at this. Better than anyone, as a matter of fact.

I can't hear you. I'm drowning in a river of guilt.

Wal-Mart puts in her two cents worth. "I see your face has cleared up just fine now."

Oh, be quiet. For some reason I thought you might be on my side.

"Our experience has led us to be suspicious when a patient with an eating disorder enters a bathroom shortly after a meal. Were you throwing up?" Atalanta questions.

I look flabbergasted. "Me? No."

Good, she doesn't have a clue.

"Were you exercising?" asks Atalanta, looking suspicious.

Oh no.

"No," I say, chuckling, "of course not." I look down, like I'm trying to spot bugs in the carpeting. Maybe Wal-Mart will help me out.

"Are you sure about that, Gary?" asks Wal-Mart, still grinning at me. "How come you seem a bit anxious all of sudden?"

Why don't you go and gather carts in the parking lot or something?

All I can think of to do is shrug my shoulders, no matter how much IT screams obscenities at me.

You good for nothing, cheating, two-faced, little—

I know, I know, you're exactly right. I'm every single one of those foul names. Why am I such a snot? It's not the real me.

"From now on, young man, you're going to have to find something to keep yourself occupied instead of pacing the floor after a meal," says Atalanta, motioning down the hall. "Go and have a seat by Chandra." Her tight lips and firm tone says she means business.

I nod and bow, like an obedient slave. That's kind of what I feel like, actually.

CHAPTER TEN

O.T.

I find myself sitting in the same chair that I've claimed every time I've been in the lounge since I got here. Force of habit. I call it My Chair. *Sports Illustrated* is my magazine of choice. I'm nuts about it. Hours are spent projecting myself into the fantasy worlds of professional athletes, particularly baseball players. My favorite is Jim Gantner, third baseman for the Milwaukee Brewers. My hometown of Eden also just happens to be Mr. Gantner's hometown. Dad regularly reminds me how Jim, when he was a kid, would shag fly balls for his legion baseball team. Jim made it to the World Series a few years ago, and put the "metropolis" of Eden (all 369 people) on the map. I wish I had Jim's body. He's young and wiry, muscular and solid, with veins sticking out of his arm like tree roots, what I consider the perfect baseball body. I wonder what it feels like. Does he feel full all the time? How much does he eat? I know it's more than me, but how much more? I wish I could eat as much as Jim and not feel guilty or fat.

It's that time again.

Yes, I think you're right. It's time for my favorite game show, Let's Be Somebody Else.

For the remainder of the day, I walk like Jim, talk like Jim, stare like Jim, lift like Jim, reach like Jim, stand like Jim, sit like Jim, jump like Jim, exercise like Jim, turn, twist, laugh, smile, comb, brush, dress, write, read, and drink like Jim. I become Jim mentally, pretending he's the one on Unit 13 with ten psychiatric patients. I get drunk on Jim. My confidence skyrockets.

Stan comments that I've been acting a little strange for the last few hours, walking bowlegged and talking a bit funny. Leonard catches me standing in front of the bathroom mirror, taking imaginary swings as if a baseball bat was in my hands.

"Are you okay, Gary?" asks Leonard. I immediately go into the motion of ringing my hands, like I just finished washing them. He even makes an attempt to feel my forehead.

"I'm fine, Leonard." I duck out before his hand touches my skin.

The following morning, I wake up with the Jim urge gone. I have a Jim hangover. If I want him back, I have to exert an incredible amount of energy, which, not to my surprise, I don't have right now. I am a nothing again.

Nothingness is too overwhelming. So, I become enthralled with another athlete, movie star, family member, friend, stranger walking past me in the mall, or any other person other than plain old me. I become aware of a person I admire, jump into a nearby phone booth in my mind and zip into their costume, and enjoy the bliss of my imagination. Even though I understand from past experiences that the thrill won't last more than a day (although I attempt to make it last), it's one day less that I have to put up with being a nothing.

But you do it so well.

A crackling, high-pitched voice startles me. "O.T., everyone, O.T."

What in the world is that? It sounds like the mating call of the white-breasted whooping crane.

"Stan, come on, let's go. O.T. everyone. Tom, Bill, turn off the soaps, it's time for O.T. Leonard, you can chat with the ladies later. Let's get a move on people."

A long-limbed, gangly woman with big glasses and a hop in her gait comes bounding down the corridor. She gathers up patients with an enthusiasm of a child snatching candy at a parade. They immediately drop what they're doing, get up, and follow this woman like zombies.

"Come on everyone. You too, Gary."

Wait a minute, how does she know my name?

We walk out of the unit and down the entrance hallway. The odors of turpentine, glue, and newsprint saturate the air. Welcome to O.T. That stands for occupational therapy, a class where patients engage in arts and crafts. The owner of the voice is Nurse Jezi, an ADHD sort of woman who apparently forgot to swallow her Ritalin this morning. She flutters around like a confused fruit bat. She's constantly in a hurry and always seems to be carrying something.

The class is awesome. Its purpose stems from the idea that emotional expression is not always forthright using verbal means. Translation: Some people talk with glue, listen with the stroke of a brush, and feel with the making of a belt.

Jezi has me pick out a pre-molded clay statue to paint. I choose bookends in the shape of a baseball and football. I pull up a chair at my usual opposite end of a table, away from the mob. They dribble around a conversation about car tires. It goes downhill after that.

"Hey, Gary," yells Jezi, cupping her hands around her mouth, "is that you down there? I don't want to have to dial long distance to reach you. Why don't you come over and join us?"

Not one to make waves by saying no, I move my project two chairs closer, still leaving one chair between me and Ida, a neurotically depressed, paranoid sprite of a woman who told us in group therapy that she chews in the neighborhood of twenty (I'm not exaggerating) packs of gum a day—a gumaholic.

"We want you to be part of our group and talk with us. What do you think about this weather? Which tire would you go with, steel-belted Road Handlers or the radical new bug-squashing Rubber Rebels?" I shrug my shoulders and bathe in quiet laughter, smiling of course.

"I don't know."

Leave me alone, please.

"Oh, come on. You gotta pick one."

Auugh! I wish I could just tell her how I—

I think not. She can't handle her own feelings.

"Honest," I say, smiling, "I really don't know."

Ida frantically unwraps three sticks of gum and thrusts them into her mouth. She reminds me of a squirrel getting ready for an early winter.

Jezi's attention is rock solid on me. "I can sense this is very difficult for you, Gary,"

"Rubber Rebels," I finally say. "I'd go with the Rubber Rebels."

There, you happy?

"How come?"

Oh, good grief. Give it a rest, woman.

"I don't know."

I turn my attention to my painting, throwing in a question about the weather every now and then to make it look like I actually want to be part of this silly conversation. Leonard suddenly gets the goofy idea that it's his responsibility to try and get me to talk. Jezi probably put him up to it.

"How are things going, Gary? It must be hard to suffer from an eating disorder," Leonard says, leaning across the table toward me.

Why does he care? You don't deserve anyone's sympathy.

"I'm okay. I hang in there."

"Now, I hope you don't go discrediting yourself from any progress you've made so far. I always tell myself to take it one day at a time. You always have another day to start fresh and new."

You think Jezi pays him by the hour?

I nod and smile.

"Take me for instance. I wish I could give you a chunk of my own weight. Eating has always been a problem with..."

The word "eating" sets off my anxiety alarm. Eating, eating, eating. Why is it such a big issue with me? I never asked for it to be this way. Why in the world does it matter how I eat, where I eat, when I eat, and what I eat if I have the "right genes"?

My mind flashes back to a scene in the kitchen at home a few years back. I came upstairs to get my third helping of ice cream. Mom was sewing at the kitchen table. I got ready to go back downstairs to watch my baseball game on television when, in the middle of cutting some fabric, she made an out-of-the-blue comment to me: "Gaa-ry! You know, if you keep eating like that you're going to get fat."

"I'm hungry."

The word is out that fat and sweets catch up with you. Don't you watch the television with all those Barbie-looking models and men with washboard abs? If you don't look like the athletes in Sports Illustrated, you'll never be happy with yourself. You're probably getting a little on the tubby side and that's her way of telling you. She's into subtle hinting, you know.

I rounded the corner to the stairway and stopped in my tracks, contemplating her stinging words one more time.

I wonder...

My voracious appetite was famous, but the reality of my developmental stage, combined with an incredibly active lifestyle, canceled out any excess calories I collected. At least I think it did. The scale and mirror in gym class did tell me the making of a spare tire was beginning to form around my waste.

See? You really aren't good enough the way you are.

So, what is it? Do I really eat too much?

I guess so.

Otherwise, why would she even make a comment like that?

I continued back downstairs with my bowl of ice cream and sat down, ready to take in another Brewers game with my dad. Just as I lifted a gooey scoop of ice cream to my lips, IT started in again.

I wouldn't do that if I were you. You're going to get fatter than you already are.

I stared at the chocolate sauce dripping off the spoon. I sighed, then set the bowl down next to my chair, never to look at food the same way again.

CHAPTER ELEVEN

SCRABBLE

"**W**elcome back," *sniff*, " welcome back." *Sniff*. "How was O.T.?" *Sniff*.

Fantastic. Thrilling. Edge-of-your-seat action every minute.

"Gary," *sniff*, "the dietician is here to see you." *Sniff*. "She's waiting for you in the dining room." *Sniff, sniff*."

I've always wanted to talk to a dietician, a fellow expert who appreciates the fine art of food diagnostics. Her name is Judy. She packs my next day's menu in hand, along with some high-tech calculator. I can't wait to find out how much I will be allowed to eat. I'm like Pavlov's dog salivating at the sound of a dinner bell. We sit down and get to work.

"Your doctor has put you on a 2,000-calorie-a-day diet."

Wha...wha...what? I need to down two grand a day? Delicious.

What do you mean delicious? Do you realize how fat you'll feel?

Yeah, but—

They'll fatten you up like a Thanksgiving turkey.

Yeah, but it's my protocol, and I can't disobey and be rude.

Protocol schmotocol.

"There's a choice of appetizer, main entrée, salad, and dessert," continues Judy. "The menu is on a three-week rotation, so you'll get plenty of variety."

Just you wait, buster. All those thigh-kicking calories...

"You have the choice of having all your calories on trays or split up in snacks throughout the day. My goal is to get you back to as normal an eating pattern for a healthy lifestyle as possible. I suggest three well-balanced meals and a snack sometime in the day."

She hands me the menu to begin my selections. I am like a child in a candy store. There are so many yummy combinations to choose from. Roast beef with mashed potatoes and gravy, fried chicken, cheesecake, creamy cheese soup, chocolate milk, the list goes on. My mouth begins to water. My stomach sounds like thunder.

Judy circles food items at my command and tallies calories on the calculator. My own involuntary, mental math machine is quicker to the trigger.

Nope, too much fat. Nope, too many calories. How about the always-scrumptious celery plate?

Well, if I have to.

Not have to—must.

I sneak a glance at Judy as I jockey back and forth, obsessing over which food combinations would give me the most pleasure to eat but the least calories and full feeling. She is being incredibly patient, I know, but I need to get this just right. It must be perfect, faultless, and ideal, to where I'm comfortable.

Ten minutes pass.

I want that soup, but soup usually settles on my stomach like asphalt. The bread tastes great with butter, but I'd be over my fat limit. I've never had raspberry torte. I'd love to try it, but the cream cheese will bloat me. What to do, what to do...

Twenty minutes.

"I'm sorry, Judy," I say apologetically. "Would you erase the chocolate milk and put two percent instead...no wait—yeah, okay, do it."

You're absolutely nuts wasting this woman's time like this.

Thirty minutes.

"What all's in your hoagie sandwiches?"

She names six different items. I calculate the exact caloric amount in five seconds. She circles, then un-circles. The pencil eraser is now worn out.

"Does the cottage cheese plate come with a half cup or whole cup of cottage cheese? Is it low-fat?"

Look at her face. She's getting perturbed at you. You need to say something to ease her distress.

"I'm sorry, Judy, for taking up so much of your time."

"That's okay, Gary. I can see this is very difficult for you. However, I will need to get going soon, so you're going to have to make up your mind."

Forty minutes.

Maybe if you scratch out bacon for breakfast…

"We are going to have to stop here, Gary. I have more visits to make before I leave today. Why don't you let me—"

"No, wait!" Wow, I sound totally panicked. Okay, calm down. "Just put me down for the…the, uh, the…okay, just give me the white toast and be done with it." I run my fingers through my hair. Judy graciously says good-bye and exits the room. I sigh.

You're a sick young man.

Bob, a tall, husky man with a jelly-looking belly, and the only male nurse on the unit, sees me sulking in My Chair.

"Why the long face, Gary?"

"Huh? Oh, nothing," I say. My eyes stay fixed on my fidgety hands. Presently, I'm deeply entrenched in another one of my bad habits—digging the fingernail of my middle finger under the nail of my thumb. It stings, but I find some kind of weird comfort in it.

Bob doesn't give up easily. He scratches his belly and looks around the room, trying to dig around in his brain for some comforting words to say. He strikes gold.

"You like games?" he asks.

No! You need to sit here and be the life of your own sulking party.

I look up, and say, "Games, well, uh—"

"Good, so do I," says Bob, walking toward the dining room, where a large closet in the corner is stuffed with board games. "Come to think of it, I think Chandra does, too. Why don't I go get her and we play?"

As long as Chandra will be there, I'll play anything.

The game is Scrabble. Bob, Chandra, and I sit in the dining room and compete. We sit for more than ninety minutes, teasing each other while making words like "bungle," "spit," "barf," and "zoos." I have to admit, I find it quite entertaining and it helps keep my mind off that menu I just butchered with Judy. The game ends with Chandra as the victor and me coming in last, of course. I rarely win at games. I think it's a sign of pending doom in my life.

Bob excuses himself to do some charting, leaving Chandra and me at the table.

"Well, that was fun," Chandra says, putting letters away. "How'd your day go?"

"Alright, I guess. Nothing too exciting to report. How about you?"

"Mine was okay, too. I found out I might be going home this weekend."

What? No. Please say you're kidding me.

"Oh, really," I say, trying to look happy for her. "Good for you."

"Yeah, I guess so."

"You don't sound too excited about it."

"Oh, like, I'm excited to get out of here and all. It's just that, like, well…"

This is getting too touchy feely. You'll freak out. Just make her feel better and get out of there.

"That's okay. You don't have to say."

"No offense or anything."

"None taken."

I turn the topic to personal interests. It turns out that Chandra is a competitive gymnast and a freshman honor student. She was an ant's eyelash away from competing at nationals last year when her eating disorders wriggled their way into her life. I spend the next half hour playing suck up, dancing my way through a superficial conversation that would impress the Secret Service.

What a fake. What a prude. What a liar.

After what seems like the longest day of my life, Unit 13 calls it quits with something known as Reflections. It's the time of day when all patients gather together in the lounge to talk about the day's events and set personal goals for tomorrow. Then it's off to bed. I brush my teeth and shut off the lights, lying with my arms folded behind my head, thinking. Thinking, thinking, thinking.

What are people at school going to think?

They'll think you're nuts.

Boy, I'm hungry...

Feels good, doesn't it?

The word has probably tapped the ears of the school's informants already...

I'm sure you'll hear about it very soon.

I could use a sandwich...

Sorry, no eating after supper.

I'm going to have so much homework to do. Will I ever be normal?

This is normal for you.

Why did this eating disorder ever happen to me?

You're terrified of growing up.

What?

CHAPTER TWELVE

THE DOCTOR IS IN(SANE)

M y top five generic good-for-all-occasions conversation zappers are (5) "Good," (4) "Fine," (3) "Okay," (2) "I'm alright," and the number one zapper, "I don't know." I use them strategically and often, hoping others will catch my drift and leave me alone. Many times my plan succeeds with the average person on the street. However, on Unit 13, I am not dealing with average.

My psychiatrist is short, pencil-thin, and topped with glossy white hair. He dresses casually, like he's on his way to do some hiking in the mountains, and has distinguished rectangular glasses that continually slide down his nose. His name is Dr. Buckmier, and he seems flakier than a blizzard in a Wheaties factory.

"Gary? Good morning, sir. I'm Dr. Buckmier. It's a pleasure to meet you. Come on down to the sun room and let's have a chat, shall we?"

We head into a tiny room just off the lounge. It's encased in large cathedral windows covered with manila-colored blinds to block out the sun. It also overlooks the hospital staff parking lot, giving it a real tourist-attraction view. We sit facing each other and engage in small talk for the first five minutes, of which I limit myself to about one minute air time. I dress myself in my Sunday-best cheerful face. Then it's down to business.

"Well," he takes a deep breath and exhales, "how are we doing today?"

"Good," I say, displaying my usual sunny smile.

There's silence. Dr. Buckmier changes his exterior from pleasant and benign to serious.

One minute passes.

Two minutes.

Two and a half.

Three minutes.

I keep staring at his hiking boots, occasionally meeting his eyes to check out where he's at. Eventually, it's back out onto the racetrack.

"How are you feeling right now?" he asks.

"Okay," I say.

We embark upon another minute of silence. This time he begins jotting something in an ugly green unit chart, one of seven scattered at his feet. I take a deep breath and exhale. The rumbling of the breakfast cart echoes in the distance.

"How are you getting along with staff and patients on the unit?"

"Fine."

He nods and puts his head down, writing earnestly as if he's completing the last sentences of an essay test.

Breakfast is waiting. Can't he write faster?

"How are you handling the decrease in exercise?"

"I'm alright."

Silence. Scribble, scribble, scribble.

"What do you intend to get out of treatment while you're here?"

"I don't know."

Done. All five responses accounted for, and in descending order, too.

"So, tell me a little bit about yourself."

No, *please* no.

Since I'm trained not to make waves, I provide him a condensed version of my life story. It takes approximately forty-five seconds. He writes frantically and babbles that we're going to take it "slow and easy" with my treatment.

In other words: No exercise class yet.

He begins his departure address. I only hear, "Blah, blah, blah, blah, blah..." My mind is too enthralled with my hotcakes getting cold in the dining room.

He rises and reaches for the doorknob. "Oh, by the way, Atalanta mentioned something to me about you anxiously pacing the unit. Since your plan calls for weight increases and limited exercise at this point, I am prescribing you to sit at least one hour after meals. It's typical unit protocol for those with eating disorders."

NOOOOOO!

"Okay, sounds good."

Finally, I hear, "Enjoy your day. It's going to be a windy one."

He certainly is.

To breakfast I go—"pancakes à la bloat." I feel like a beached whale forty-five minutes later, which is my record time on the unit for eating a meal so far. My stomach distends and feels like I've swallowed battery acid. I rarely ever get pancakes at home. I love the taste, but I kick myself for ever putting the stupid things on my fork. I add up the damage: 600 calories, more than I typically eat in an entire twenty-four hour period on many days. My lament carries forth in My Chair afterward:

Oh, thy breading being bloating, syrup thy stomach coating.

Thou dost eat them together for thine intestinal groaning.

What shall become of thee before thou ever wilt learn?

Never let thy yearnings lead or thy gullet shall churn.

Self-discipline must be thy rule of thumb,

Without it let thee be condemned to thine ordinary chum.

Shakespeare and I never got along.

At least Chandra will be next to me, whenever she gets here. I look up and spot her sneaking down the corridor in a rush, anxiously looking over her shoulder as if being followed. She plops into a chair next to me, breathing heavily.

"In a hurry are we?"

"Yeah, I wanted to get my journal before Atalanta saw me. She didn't see me, did she?"

"Not that I know of."

She opens up a neon purple notebook and begins writing spiritedly with a frilly-topped pen. Judging by the thickness of the rippled, written-on pages, she's almost finished a novel.

"I actually got the idea from Greta," says Chandra. "It helps me organize the mess going on in my head, kind of like a diary. She said it's a good way to remind myself that my thoughts and feelings are okay."

"Does it work?"

"Yeah, sort of. I love writing anyhow. How about you?"

"Well, I don't know. I've always liked language arts but, well, I, uh... I guess my family has never been much for reading or writing."

My thoughts flounder in the amalgam pasted to the walls of my stomach. Syrup is sappy, not fizzy, so burping is out of the question. I watch game shows and skim through year-old copies of *Crazy about Psychiatry* magazine. Chandra writes in earnest.

You're so fat.

I push out my abdomen against my jogging pants elastic and look down. It looks like a beer gut. I feel terrible.

You could have thrown up.

It's during moments like this that I do a tailspin into the wall of my conscience, singing of everything bad and abysmal about my wretched body. Nothing anyone can say or do will make me happy. I can't take the food away.

I've lost control. I'm a failure. I am—what do you mean throw it up?

Bulimia, remember? You read about it in a book Greta gave you.

Observation hour expires. I immediately visit the bathroom and delve into an array of cardiovascular movement, hoping to rid my body of a few unwanted calories in the process.

It's hopeless. You can't burn calories fast enough. You might as well stop. Unless, of course, you— It will go faster.

I pause, contemplating the action I am about to attempt. Gosh, this is hard. I'll try it one more time... Nope, it's not working. How am I going to make it through this?

Change your menu selections for tomorrow. They're up at the front desk.

I take off on my assignment. The *Mission Impossible* theme echoes in my head.

"Howdy, Gary," says Wal-Mart. "How can I help you?"

"Could I see my menu again, please? I forgot to circle something."

Surprisingly, she coughs it up. I cross out bacon and eggs and circle two cereals for breakfast. My movement is swift in order to finish in a timely manner before Atalanta or Hadie figure out what's going on. I finish and stuff it back into the pack of other menus.

"Thanks, Wal—I mean, Samantha."

"No problem, hon."

Mission accomplished.

Are you sure you marked it correctly?

Oh, no! I marked the wrong one! I wonder if I... No, it's too late now. Auuuugh!

Chapter Thirteen

Send the Alternate

I've just gotten word from Mom that I've been selected to prom court. It's less than two weeks away. How come me? Who voted me in? Yes, I'm flattered but I don't want to go. I'd be working triple time in the impress department. I can't do it—no way, no how. Send the alternate. What's his phone number?

They probably just feel sorry for you.

This should be exciting news. Why do I feel like my life is backwards?

Other people feel relieved by a satisfied stomach; I find it despicable. Other people find peer parties pleasurable; I find them frightening. Other people's crabbiness disappears after eating when they're hungry; my grouchiness shows up when I'm full. Other people confidently express a genuine identity; I seem to have misplaced mine. Other people long to go home from the psych unit; I can think of no other place I'd rather be right now. Other people—

That's because you're odd, a freak of nature.

At school, the extent of my social output stretches only to the cafeteria, where I have reduced myself to idle background, like a department store mannequin. I typically enter the school cafeteria alone, give a friendly wave to my former popular following, and nestle myself at the far end of the lunch table with my half a PBJ sandwich and skim milk. I read a little clip of baseball box scores I cut out of the paper that morning. I give off an aura that screams, "Leave me alone! Let the leper eat in peace." It's a custom my friends have learned to respect.

It wasn't always this way. During freshman year, I was simply one of the guys, your regular, garden-variety Mr. Popular: smart, athletic, charming, lots of friends. In the cafeteria, I used to be in the thick of my friends, talking sports, girls, and whether or not we were going out for pizza after football practice. I passed through the lunch line asking the cooks to load my plate high with anything they could reach.

Something happened toward the end of freshman year. IT had been part of my conscience for years up to that point, but never seemed to bother me that much. I don't know exactly how IT started; it was always just there. IT somehow grabbed my attention, like someone rudely tugging on my ear. I found myself moving farther and farther down the lunch table, away from my friends. I quit going through the lunch line like a ravenous shark and began brown-bagging my lunch, which I quickly reduced to nothing more than an apple. It was a subtle move at first, and people didn't make anything of it.

IT blared loudly in my ear in all its glory, saying things like: *You don't really believe you're as great at sports as your peers say you are, do you? I mean, come on, you're going to screw up and let them down sooner than later...*

You're getting tired of putting on this I'm-happy-and-all-put-together act, aren't you? That cheerleader who has a crush on you will never go for the real you in a million years. She'll sniff out how fake you are before your first date. Speaking of dating, what if she wants to have sex?

If you want to compete with professional athletes someday, you're going to have to do something about that pathetic-looking body of yours. You see what these elite athletes in Sports Illustrated look like and how they train.

High school won't last forever; you're going to need to figure out what in the world you want to do with your ridiculously shallow life. People are watching you, and taking notes on you, and expecting you to be this remarkable success.

Why don't you come up with something to avoid ever having to deal with any of these unnecessary pressures. Hey, you know what? I have just the thing...

I was sickly insecure inside, confused over my true identity, and horrified of feelings. My life shifted into third gear and crashed into the ditch after that. Then a thought occurred to me: What if, for some strange reason, I should happen to trade in this heavy burden around my neck for a more adventurous, spontaneous, creative lifestyle? IT immediately put me in my place.

People might get confused and think you're crazy, especially your father. You're supposed to be the second coming of Jim Gantner, remember?

Don't remind me.

You're next in line.

Send the alternate—*please.*

CHAPTER FOURTEEN

THE BATTLE OF O.T.

"I heard you have a special day coming up soon, Gary," says Jezi while teaching a patient how to knit. "What are your plans?"

How did she find out? Oh, yeah, the scuttlebutt runs thick up here: It's called "weekly staffing meetings."

"Nothing special." I keep my head down and look intent on finishing up the paint job on my sporty bookends. O.T. is really growing on me.

"Well, happy birthday, Gary. That's wonderful."

Oh, great, here we go.

"Oh, come on, Gary," Jezi pushes. "You have to do something to let your hair down once in a while. You're too much of a hermit."

What's wrong with that?

"Invite some friends over. Go out on the town. Stay up all night."

I smile and nod as always. I have never stayed up all night in my life, nor have I dated, been to a party with peers of any kind, or experimented with drugs, alcohol, or tobacco. It's too risky, too defeating. If I chose to dabble in anything even remotely controversial, I would let too many people down. They wouldn't think I'm the great all-American boy that they think I am.

This reputation is murder to maintain.

Perfection is the goal. Remember that.

I don't know. Are you sure there is such a thing? I mean, I've been—

Keep going. You'll get there.

My plaster bookends are just about complete. Then I graduate to making one of those cool belts I see Leonard designing and staining. I'll make one for Dad. He'd like that. My stomach twists and turns from the hoagie sandwich I ate for lunch. All I can think about is the bologna, the three slices of cheese, the mayonnaise, the cottage cheese plate with canned fruit—all 652 calories worth. I want to perform surgery on my intestines to take out what's inside.

You've got to exercise. You need to move.

I push myself away from the table and browse through the cabinets, pretending to be searching for a leather belt.

Remain standing. It will burn more calories.

A few minutes pass.

"Gary, dear, come on back over to the table. Your belt is ready to go," Jezi calls. "You can start with the punch-out tools."

I walk back over to the table but remain standing, looking for interesting shapes to engrave into my belt. I stand and look, stand and hammer, stand and stain, stand and stretch, stand and toss garbage away.

"Why don't you have a seat?" says Jezi, politely but pointedly.

"I want to stretch my legs. I get tired of sitting all day."

"This is part of your obsessive–compulsive tendencies with your eating disorder, isn't it?"

What? Well, no I—

"Sit, Gary."

Draw your sword.

Schwwwwing!

"Really, Jezi, I'd like to stand for just a little while."

Jezi puts down a punch-out tool and looks up at me, grinning as if her picture is just about to be taken. "Gary, I'm not going to tell you again. Please have a seat."

Don't move.

What am I doing? This is not me. It's too uncomfortable for my taste. I hate confrontation.

Not when someone sticks their nose in your control.

I look down, ignoring Jezi, playing tug-of-war with guilt. I'm losing.

The room is silent, the rest of the patients tapping away at their belt projects. Jezi straightens up. "One..." She begins walking around the table. "Two..."

My stomach is a mass of twisted knots.

Jezi gently rests her hands on my shoulders. "Three..." and forces me down into a chair. "That's better. You're a stubborn coot, aren't you?" She begins assisting the patient next to me.

Without skipping a beat, I reflexively fall into a ritual of tightening and releasing my abdominal muscles, forcing small twists to each side. At the same time, I extend my legs out in isometric contractions, then release. Jezi feels the air whooshing beneath the table from my legs whipping up and down.

"*Gaa*-ry..." she says, turning to me with a raised eyebrow and a grin.

She's beginning to sound like your mother.

I turn red and cease the leg workout.

She can't see you tighten your tummy.

My stomach muscles burn like fire, followed by a sharp pain. I think I just tore a muscle.

After five repetitions, Jezi announces that it's time to line up and head back to the unit. Darn, I have five more sets to do. I guess I can finish in My Chair while watching *Gilligan's Island.*

I chart my course directly for the lounge and reach to turn on the TV. I turn around and almost run into my parents.

"Hi, Gary," says Mom, awkwardly fumbling with a pile of books under arm. "How's it going? Here's the homework Rick brought home for you today. He says your teachers are all pulling for you. They don't want you to overwork yourself, so just do what you can."

You're eliciting sympathy from teachers. See, I'm your best friend.

Dad wanders the lounge, intrigued by the craftsmanship of the ceiling beams.

I give them the lowdown of my day and ask my dad if he'd like to play Ping–Pong once he finishes staring at the ceiling. My body craves movement. We end up whacking the ball around for about forty minutes. Bob makes a dozen trips up and down the corridor, observing me like a hawk, charting my every blink. I stretch, bend, swing, reach, and twist with great fervor, expending as much energy as possible. I could go all night.

Go hard. Burn all the gas you can. You need to get up two times tonight to exercise, too. Tomorrow is roast pork and gravy.

I quickly discover that Ping–Pong is fun. I don't understand it, but it's really a blast. Who would have ever imagined a simple little game would be so exhilarating.

It burns calories, plain and simple.

Yeah, whatever.

Hey, watch your tone with me, mister.

For brief episodes during our play, I am free. There's no IT, no guilt, no obsessing about food, calories, or weight—only uninhibited fun. It feels refreshing, like a cool drink of water splashing over my parched throat. But, as usual, slowly worming its way between this father-and-son Kodak moment...

It must be earned. Fun will only be allowed if calories are being extinguished.

But, but—

No buts.

I sigh. Yes, sir.

My play suddenly gets squashed to obsessing over how full I'm going to feel at dinner in a matter of hours. I step my Ping–Pong game up another notch, but not because I want to have more fun; I need to burn another hundred calories to equal the slice of buttered bread that will complement the rest of my dinner, which will be exactly 837 calories. Actually, no, it will be 896 calories because I ordered the orange juice, too—No wait a minute, that's for tomorrow's breakfast. Tonight's dinner has apple juice, which has six fewer calories, so that brings my caloric count—

BOINK!

"Oops, sorry about that, Gary," says Dad, as I rub my forehead after being stung by the Ping–Pong ball. "You better pay attention."

Yes, keep paying attention to what you're doing. Now, let's see, you were at 834 calories...

CHAPTER FIFTEEN

WHAT ABOUT BOB?

"Gary," says Bob, interrupting me during an exciting episode of *Wheel of Fortune*. "How about you and I have a little chat? I'd like to touch base with you before you go to sleep."

"Okay."

We head into the group room. There's an eerie quiet when Bob shuts the door.

"So," says Bob, taking a seat directly in front of me, "how's it going this evening?"

"Pretty good, I guess." I keep my distance, but not too far away so as not to be impolite.

"I understand you're quite the ball player."

"Yeah..."

What's going on here?

I smile and quickly rattle off all pertinent information to satisfy his investigative urges. At first I do most of the talking, controlling the direction of the conversation. But then I slide over to the passenger seat and follow Bob's lead, carefully planning my words, tone of voice, and facial expressions, trying to be kind as possible and please him at all times. I'm reminded of a verse I learned in church: Love thy neighbor as thyself.

That's love thy neighbor instead of yourself.

Oh, yeah? Well, how come when I looked it up in the Bible it said—

Thou shalt look at it my way.

Oh.

"You know, Gary, it's okay to tell me how you feel," Bob says, interrupting my internal dialogue. "I won't break."

What the—? Where did this come from?

"I know. I'm doing okay, really."

He shoots me a thoughtful stare as if to say, "Yeah, right."

"So tell me," he says casually, leaning back in his chair, "how do you go about training for baseball?"

Boy, you're desperate for conversation, aren't you?

"Dad hits me ground balls regularly," I explain, yawning at the same time. It's another opportunity to impress someone with my exhausting schedule. "I hit off my batting tee about ten to twelve hours a week, and we have regular practices for the team in summer. I also spend hours every week throwing tennis balls off the side of our garage to practice my defense. Then there's dozens of wind sprints every morning—rain, snow, or shine—to maintain my speed. I do weight training daily and year round for strength conditioning and do various stretching exercises specifically designed for baseball players."

You know, you really need to add more strenuous exercises to these wimpy baseball workouts. You'll singe more calories, and feel the pain in your muscles for a much longer period of time.

"Wow, that's impressive. I suppose it has really improved your game."

"Well, yeah..."

No, it hasn't, actually.

"It's interesting," continues Bob. "You work yourself to the bone with this training routine, but your weight and strength have decreased over time."

You know, come to think of it, my speed has decreased as well and—

Don't let him trick you by putting words into you mouth.

There's a stiff silence. Anger engorges my core, or is it embarrassment? It's hard to tell.

"You got rather quiet all of a sudden," says Bob.

"I'm just thinking."

"What about?"

What's going on inside me? I want to bellow obscenities right now. What do I do? What do I say? He's got me in a corner. I'm a little mouse that got suckered into snuffling some peanut butter, and now I'm stuck in the trap. How do I maneuver my way out?

Diffuse him.

"I guess I'm not used to talking about myself like this," I mumble. "I don't know what to say."

Bob leans forward on his knees. "Say what you're thinking. Be honest. Feel your feelings. Let them out. They're not going to hurt you or me."

Yes, they will.

"I guess I'm feeling frustrated."

Good. That's one of those generic feeling words. Less controversial.

"How so?" inquires Bob, looking at me with the utmost curiosity.

"I don't know. I can't make heads or tails of anything. I feel trapped. I just want it to end."

Be careful now.

A mishmash of ideas gets all mangled up inside my head like Christmas tree lights stuffed in a box. I want to express true emotion and be honest in my opinions, but, well, I—I—I just can't. Maybe these are my genuine thoughts. I don't know. My anger intensifies.

Don't look into his eyes. You're not going to like it. You're disappointing him.

I sigh heavily and squeeze the arms of my chair, looking at the wall over his shoulder. Bob remains silent and still.

Just keep your eyes straight ahead. Focus on that fly flitting around on the wall.

"You're okay, Gary. You're okay." Bob brings his face to within inches of mine. He taps my knee. "You are dealing with a lifetime of emotional baggage. Change will not happen overnight. It takes time. But the more you are willing to open up and express genuine emotion, and not just label the feeling, the quicker your recovery will be."

What do you mean, recovery? As if that's possible.

I look away. I can't betray my best friend. IT has brought me too much security.

Not long after, realizing I'm not going to take the bait, Bob raises his white flag and surrenders. We leave the room. My underarms are soaked. I'm relieved to be done with that uncomfortable conversation, but I sense that a golden chance at hope is lost. Bob opens a window of opportunity for me to express my feelings in a safe, peer-free environment and, instead of taking advantage of it, I flippantly toss it back out of the window.

You made your own bed. Now lie in it.

I just can't win, can I?

I sense evil snickering.

CHAPTER SIXTEEN

MY FREE GET-OUT-OF-PROM CARD

*Huff...huff...huff...huff...*I hope, *huff...huff*—that the third shift nurses—*huff...huff...huff*—don't break—*huff...huff*—their rounds routine—*huff...huff...huff...*

The time is two o'clock in the morning. I'm flat on my back in bed after three uninterrupted minutes of high knee kicking. Off I press into my lower abdominal series. Ouch! I'm still working through the pain from the muscle I tore during O.T. I stiffen my body, and raise my straightened legs off the bed about six inches. I hold...hold...hold ...one firm minute, then rest. Ten more are ahead of me.

Two nurses do the graveyard shift. I observed them peeking in my door at the top of every hour last night. I schedule my moonlight workout accordingly. Excuse me, I need to hit the floor. One, two, three, four, five...only 195 push-ups to go. Twenty minutes later, after karate kicking and punching, I flop back on my bed.

You've earned your sleep—for now.

Three hours later, my eyelids pop open. Shoot. I forgot to set my alarm for my second workout.

Get back on schedule. Let's go.

Sniffer Hadie does my weigh in. I'm anxious to see how much I lost while slaving away at exercise last night. This should be good. I should probably weigh— What the—?

You didn't do enough.

What a rip-off. All that suffering. All that wasted sleep. All for a *two-pound gain*. It's times like these that I get to thinking whether or not all this exercising and pain is worth it.

Don't question me. Just obey.

Dr. Buckmier intercepts me on my way out of the exam room. "We have bright sunshine this morning, Gary. Let's come on down here, shall we? It's a cheery sunny day out there, and the birds are chirping an enchanted melody."

Oh, brother.

We reach the sunroom and take our positions. He carries on for another few minutes with a story about how his son dropped a fly ball during a baseball game yesterday. I smell a metaphor for life disappointment coming on. I just practice my endurance smiling and say "Oh, really?" and "I see" every now and then to keep his motor going. It's less time focused on my issues. Approximately seven minutes later, his chit-chat gauge hits empty.

"So, how are we doing today?"

Let's begin with the generic top five.

"Good."

Silence takes its turn again. I hate this. It's such a waste of time.

Let's see, what will be coming up for meals tomorrow?

"I see your weight was up a pinch today."

A pinch? More like a handful.

"Yeah."

For once, Dr. Buckmier stays speechless, content to simply stare at me with an eager grin.

I follow suit.

He scratches a few notes in my chart. What could he possibly be writing about?

Maybe he's writing an apology letter to his son for laughing at him when he dropped the fly ball. Don't forget to stick it in his lunch box, Doc.

You know, I can't tell you how much I'm really getting sick and tired of your rude attitude. I have a mind to—

To what? Let go of me? Ha, ha, ha. That's a laugh.

"How are your days going up here so far?"

"Pretty good."

Silence.

"I think it's time to start you out on something—to get the ball rolling a bit, an antidepressant called amitriptyline. It will help you get through the weight gains."

Not if I can help it. You don't do drugs.

"Okay," I reply, smiling.

"Well, then," he says, opening the door to another patient eager to see him, "you have yourself a cheery day today. The sun is shining brightly, and so is my heart." I depart the sunroom and sit back in My Chair, wishing I could take a nap. The three hours of sleep I had last night is beginning to catch up with me.

This is going to cost your parents more of their hard-earned cash. Oh, that's right, you can't help it.

I sigh, *without* a smile this time.

You're a useless waste of your parents' time and money, you know that?

Leave me alone. I'm tired.

You're not allowed to rest. You haven't earned it yet.

Aw, come on. I've been working really hard.

I let out a long, lip-stretching yawn and rest my chin in my hand. I stare blankly at nurses coming and going at the front desk. I want to disagree with IT but I'm scared to find out what happens if I put that wish into action. If only I had the courage to try, the motivation to take the risk.

Hah, I'd like to see you try, mister.

I don't know, I have a feeling one of these days I'm going to throw caution to the wind and... and...

A much-needed nap wrestles my eyelids closed. Seconds later, I'm snoring.

I'm awakened with a nudge, and a familiar sniff. "Gary?" *Sniff.* "Wake up sleepy head." *Sniff.* "You have a visitor." *Sniff.*

It's my guidance counselor, Ms. Wheeler. She brings me glad tidings of great joy from the staff at my high school: I have just been selected to be my high school's Badger Boy state representative. It's a distinguished honor given to one junior boy and girl annually who best exemplify the character qualities of citizenship, sportsmanship, leadership, and academic excellence.

Me? Why would anyone pick me? I get the feeling that I'm probably an alternate, sitting in for one of our class big wigs who refused to go because it interrupted his track meet, Bandorama concert, forensics meet, one-act play, exchange-student trip, or student-council potluck.

"You were a unanimous selection, Gary, something we haven't had in a number of years."

They just felt sorry for you, that's all.

You really think so? As I think about, maybe they really do like me for—

Nonsense. You're a fake and they know it.

"Wow!" I say, feeling slightly proud and a bit baffled. "I don't know what to say."

"Badger Boy is an event held at a private university where kids from all over the state come together to learn the ins and outs of government and about the game of politics," Ms. Wheeler adds.

Great. Here comes another people-pleasing fiesta—with strangers no less. I'm already set to get out of prom. I don't need another headache to fret about.

I hand her the completed homework I slaved over for the last few days. She thanks me by plopping at least two more weeks of homework on top of my award certificate and tells me not to worry about getting it all done this week.

"The staff wants you to concentrate on getting better first. Speaking of which," she squirms uncomfortably in her chair, "we have decided that if you are not discharged by this coming Friday, we will need to go with the alternate for prom."

Yaaaahhhhhoooooooooooo!

"I hope you're not too disappointed," she says quickly. "We all hope you can get out of here before then, especially the kids."

Sure they do. You'd be the star of the show, food for gossip, the gawk of the night.

I'd probably be the subject of more whispers and finger pointing than the time one of our school's prized cheerleaders was "discovered" in the boy's bathroom—wearing only half her uniform and in a compromising position.

No doubt.

"Well," says Ms. Wheeler, gathering up her things, "I better get going. I'll bring the good news of your steady progress back to everyone at school."

I appear discouraged to downplay the mood. It's hard to do when I'm screaming with excitement on the inside. I need to make sure I'm not out of here by prom time.

Chapter Seventeen

Chandra's Discharge

Well, I have good news and bad news. Which one do you want to hear first? The good news? Oh, really? Not me. I like to get the hard parts over first, just like I've always been told: "Work comes before play." The bad news is that I've gained almost seven pounds in the last three weeks. It's also Saturday morning, which means no group therapy, no O.T., no afternoon classes, and no exercise class. Even though these classes get a little boring, they give me something to do during my lackluster days. To be honest though, *all* of the classes are starting to grow on me, not just O.T. I don't know if I like that.

And now the good news: Since I've gained weight, Dr. Buckmier gave me the thumbs-up to join exercise class on Monday. I'm excited, but also depressed. All I can think about is seven whole pounds. Exercise will be great, but I've been sort of getting used to this sitting around business. I'm realizing I can handle it.

No, you can't. I think that nap you fell victim to did something to that tiny brain of yours. Think how fat you feel all the time.

Exercise does make me feel good. Then again, I detest doing it. Deep down I'd rather be doing something else with my time, something more... fun. I should be happy, right? I am happy. Well, not exactly...I think. I don't know.

Make up your mind.

I need to get my mind on something more pleasant.

Chandra comes and sits by me before breakfast. Today is her big day. Her cheery giddiness doesn't fool me. Something seems...off. I've seen it all before—in myself. The more time I hang up here, the sharper my radar becomes, particularly to the nuances of eating disorder armaments. There's an anxious look about her, a hesitant hook in her tone, decreased eye contact, a crinkly brow immediately preceding her speech.

She's in disguise.

We've gotten to know each other fairly well since becoming chair-bound twins after meals. We've discussed all sorts of topics: family, school, friends, movies, exercise horror stories, and dieting tips. Her status as a national-caliber gymnast requires her to attend special training out of state. Her report card carries all mountain-peak letters, she's queen bee on the social scene, ridiculously pretty, and could do commercials for acne cream—as the "after" picture.

I am going to miss Chandra around here something awful. I desperately want her to like me, to think I'm "a catch."

We're summoned for chow. Scrambled eggs with bacon blanket my plate. Chandra munches on her oatmeal and whole-wheat toast. I can tell it still pains her to be eating. She's gained more than ten pounds in her month and a half on the unit. This scares me. How much will I need to gain before they let me go? She stares down in deep contemplation. Bites are slow and laborious. A sigh or two precedes the shovel to the mouth.

I break the silence. "I'm going to miss you around here."

Come on. Chew faster. I need an answer.

"I'll miss you too," she mumbles dryly, dragging her toast around her tray like a toy.

Yesssss!

"If there's ever a time you'd like to talk, just give me a call," I say, trying to keep her talking.

"Yeah, okay." She continues to stare blankly without much expression.

It's obvious that her mind is elsewhere and she probably wants to be left alone, but I'm desperate. It's a selfish moment.

"You have my number, right?"

"I've got your number already, okay?" yells Chandra, slam dunking her toast into her orange juice. She grabs her tray, shoves it deep into the cart, and storms to her room. Bob follows in her wake.

Nice going, idiot. Now look what you've done.

My stomach feels like I just swallowed something moldy, and I don't think it's from my banana and corn flakes.

I labor through the rest of my breakfast, then go to sit in *my* chair in the lounge, sulking. What an imbecile I am.

You've got that right.

I feel terrible. How could I do that to my friend? Hadie comes and sits next to me. I wish to be left alone.

"How are you feeling, Gary?" *Sniff.*

Oh, great! Who invited you to my pity party?

"Good." I toss her a quick, customary smile.

"Chandra didn't sound too happy." *Sniff.* She's got quite a temper." *Sniff.*

I stay quiet.

"You know, I remember a time when I was a little girl and—"

Oh, no! Here it comes again. I'd rather be gutting whales in the Arctic than suffering through another one of these "When I was your age" speeches. I'm not listening. My mind is rummaging around in the mucky swamp of self-analysis. What should have I said to Chandra? How come she's so agitated this morning? How am I going to fix this situation?

Hadie finally gets up and annoys another patient for a while. I sit and gnaw a couple of my fingernails until my fingertips are raw. Chandra is now standing at the front desk with her mother, taking care of the last-minute details of discharge. I nonchalantly drift to the bathroom nearby to try to salvage a last good-bye from Chandra and get in a quick mini-workout. Greta goes over the exit arrangements and paperwork. Chandra has been pacing around the last few days like a caged panther. She wants out. At least, I think so. I sit and watch the action from a nearby bench. While awaiting her moment of truth, Chandra turns around and spots me.

She comes over and sits.

"Well, I guess this is good-bye," she says, smiling sweetly but looking like a lost puppy.

"What's the matter?"

Something is wrong again. I wish she'd tell me. Why doesn't she want to talk to me?

Maybe it's because you never really talk to her, or anyone for that matter.

Hmmm.

"I want to apologize for snapping at you earlier," says Chandra.

I suddenly feel as if a huge weight dropped from my shoulders and I can stand up straight again.

"It's just that I'm a little nervous about handling things at home on my own."

"But you won't be alone," I say encouragingly. "You'll have family and friends, plus your therapy appointments I'm sure."

"Yeah, well..." She looks unconvinced for a moment, then inhales a deep breath and lets it out forcefully, psyching herself up. "Maybe I'll get the chance to visit sometime. We could play Scrabble or something."

"That would be great."

She hesitates, but then gives me a loose hug, which gradually grows tighter...and longer. I close my eyes and savor every last moment of her touch. Too soon, she marches out the door with suitcase in hand, her mother's arm flanked around her shoulder. She looks back at me one more time before she disappears down the corridor.

My heart snaps in two.

CHAPTER EIGHTEEN

MY POST-PROM

M y alarm awakens me with an awful blaring that would resurrect the dead. I quickly slam the snooze button and roll over, exhausted. For once I didn't want to wake up early this morning. I'm still exhausted from the clandestine exercise routine I completed just a few short hours ago. Some nights, I'm so tired that I'm afraid I won't hear the alarm and will have my illicit plan exposed. At home, I would rise at 3:30 or 4:00 in the morning seven days a week, so my body was trained to wake itself early—I just want to make sure I'll be one hundred percent error free.

What I would give to be like my younger brother, Rick, who stays out late with his friends on Friday night, sleeps in on Saturday, goes to work, comes home for dinner, goes out again with friends, stays out until early-morning hours, and gets up at 7:55 on Sunday morning—five minutes before we leave for church.

Yes, it's fun to dream...Chunky! Drop and give me twenty.

After my three-minute workout in the bathroom, I head down to the lounge with my *Sports Illustrated* to gape at the same pictures and daydream of being the same people I'm not. The unit is dark and quiet. I don't believe the rooster has crowed yet. I turn to my Jim Gantner article. The pages are all crinkly and worn from my flipping through them dozens of times. All the corners are wrinkled from my nasty habit of sticking them under my fingernails until the quick of my finger is pushed back or begins to bleed. This hurts, but it also feels good in an odd sort of way.

I come across something in the picture I haven't noticed before. A man in the crowd along the first base side is holding up a sign with something written on it. I squint closely to see what it says. Written in thick black script is "Rom. 12:2." I've seen "John 3:16" numerous times held up by fans on poster board while watching the Milwaukee Brewers games on television with Dad. It's usually held high above the head of some loony lark dancing around in his seat with poofy rainbow hair and a bushy mustache and beard. He's typically being given dirty stares from fans surrounding him.

Well, as long as I have the time, I think I'll go dig myself up a Bible and—hey, who's that?

A cluster of people enters the unit at the front desk. Ariel, a lively, regular third-shift nurse who does rounds religiously at the top of every hour, is happily surprised by this young posse of people. After a brief security question-and-answer session, they all do an about face and make their way down the hallway. Familiar physiques and faces wearing formal attire come into view.

Oh. My. Goodness.

The prom court has come to pay me a visit.

A wave of terror washes over my bow. I am thoughtless, speechless, and numb. I'm not prepared for this. Look at all these people I need to please. Quick, where are my masks? Oh, here they are. Ten teens smile and stand before me.

"Gary! How are you doing?"

"How's it going, Gary?"

"Hey, buddy."

"It's great to see you, Gary."

"Whaaazzzz up?"

The others simply gaze around the unit like they're about to be attacked by a flock of wild geese.

"Hey, everyone," I say enthusiastically. "What're you all doing here?"

"We're heading out for breakfast and we were wondering if you'd like to come along with us," says Lizzy Banks, who would have been my date for the evening.

"Uh…"

"We checked at the desk and they already said no. Bummer."

Whew! That was close.

"Darn it," I say with a snap of my fingers. "That would have been great to get away from this horrible hospital food."

"Here, Gary," says Lizzy, "I brought you these. I thought they might help you feel better about missing prom." She lays a prom program, a flower, and a balloon in my lap. She looks stunning with her hair all done up. I can tell that it's since come down a tad from last night's festivities, but it still looks beautiful. She had a huge crush on me during freshman year, asking me out at least a handful of times. I said no each time—something I now regret.

You would never have a chance with her anyhow. You're not in her league. She's a cheerleader after all. You're not capable of dating a cheerleader. The guys she hangs with are all popular, good looking, athletic, and able to charm a snake out of a rat hole.

I am terrified of anyone, particularly girls, getting too close to the insecure me. Yet, I would love to enjoy a romantic affair. On the other hand, a relationship would throw a monkey wrench into the smooth-burning, well-oiled engine of my exercise and diet practices.

They would reject you. It's for the best.

Yeah. You're right. Then again, she did ask me out repeatedly.

After ten minutes of reminiscing down Prom Lane, the court gives me handshakes or hugs and disappears down the corridor.

You are an idiot. You're throwing your years away. Look what you're missing? Look at the fun you're missing.

I sigh.

How pitiful can you be?

I'm getting so sick of hearing this.

CHAPTER NINETEEN

LET'S PLAY HIDE THE TUNAFISH—TWICE

It's 9:00 p.m., time for my nighttime snack. What's this? Look at all this tuna slathered with mayonnaise. I specifically requested that my sandwich snacks not include mayonnaise. Can't anyone follow through with a simple request? There must be a sub on duty.

"I understand you need to eat this with staff supervision," says Dora, the nurse working a last-minute fill-in for Bob.

This has potential. Do your job.

"Well, as long as they can see me, it's okay. They don't have to sit right next to me."

She pulls up a chair and starts throwing questions at me. I employ my five generic responses to keep the conversation short. I need to unload some excess mayonnaise from this sandwich. Dora continues rummaging in small talk. I persist in my goal of getting rid of her. I need a plan. Oh, I know...

"Could I have some ketchup please?" I ask, showing my dimples.

"Ketchup? I, uh..."

"They usually keep it in the kitchenette room behind you."

Good, she's gullible.

I don't know about this. It seems like an underhanded trick to play.

Those are the only ones that work. Now be quiet and do your duty.

Dora opens up the kitchenette door while continuing her barrage of questions in an attempt to bond with me. I've succeeded with the first part of my mission: Operation Tunafling. I place a napkin on my lap and wait for my cue to strike.

"Where did you say they keep the ketchup?"

This is too easy.

"I think it's in the refrigerator," I reply, hands perched at the ready like a tiger prepared to pounce on a poor unsuspecting gazelle.

She pulls the refrigerator door open and bends down to scan its contents.

Now!

I take my plastic knife and scrape at least two tablespoons of mayonnaise off my sandwich and mash it into my napkin.

She's slow with her investigation. Keep going.

I cut off half my sandwich and stuff it—Oh, no! I have no pockets.

Quick! Do something before she sees!

I frantically shove it down the front of my pants.

Wow, creative.

Crumbs fall into my groin. Whoa! Now that feels weird.

"Here you go," says Dora, handing me two small packages of ketchup. Is two enough?"

"Plemfy. Fank you." I make like I stuffed the entire half of the sandwich in my mouth, puffing out my cheeks like I'm playing Chubby Bunny. Ketchup goes on the other half. Ketchup on tuna? Nasty! I should have asked for mustard. But I must follow through now.

After downing the other half of the sandwich in front of Dora's watchful eye, I scurry back to my room and bury the evidence deep inside the wastebasket under a wad of crumpled paper to keep housekeeping from discovering it.

I hope there's more gullible staff like her up here.

I get to sleep much faster this evening knowing I have fewer tuna calories settling under my skin. That means fewer calories to figure out how to burn between now and tomorrow's breakfast.

The next morning brings day thirty-three at the Unit 13 Hilton. I have memorized the three-week menu rotation. It's gotten to the point where I am mentally scheduling two, sometimes three days of meals ahead of time. This brings comfort and security to me. I know exactly what to expect for calories and can spend my energies elsewhere.

The staff is getting more intent on "getting me out of here." They encourage me to take advantage of more passes, particularly with friends my own age. I don't want to. It's too risky.

I've gotten the okay from Dr. Buckmier to roam downtown during the day. It's only a twenty-minute walk and gets me off the unit and out and about with people. That's what they want me to do, hang out with more people, improve my social skills. I prefer the hermit life.

What's wrong with it anyway? Why do we have to be around others so much?

You are not okay the way you are.

My weight is up to almost 125 pounds. The experts say I'm supposed to be feeling happier by now. But I don't believe the experts ever had an eating disorder. Staff and patients allude to the idea that I must be getting excited about going home soon, or how happy I must be over how well my recovery is going. I can't disappoint them, so I agree. Cows will serve tea before I express a sincere opinion of mine that might constitute a debate. But I crave what Unit 13 has to offer—good food, consistent structure and follow through, safety from real world responsibilities and pressures, and people who listen to me.

Rick has a basketball game at the high school. He's really good—he won all-conference MVP last year and led the league in scoring and rebounding. His presence is feared by pretty much anyone in the league.

Usually, my brother doesn't say much to me and stays to his own business, but once in a while he'll let out a "What the heck is wrong with you? Just eat and have it over with." I feel two inches tall during moments like that. Mom told me that, at one time, Rick admired me. Not anymore.

You're such an embarrassment to the family.

We get to the gymnasium for the big game. My classmates are at the other end of the bleachers. I'm packing a Unit 13 snack under my sweatshirt—a tuna fish sandwich and an apple. How humiliating is that?

Hadie sniffs at me on my way out the door before my parents picked me up, and says, "It's unit protocol, Gary. You must eat it at your regular night snack time."

I tucked my plastic hospital identification bracelet under my sweatshirt sleeve. My parents sit next to me.

"Hey, Gary," says Mom, "aren't those your friends over there? Why don't you go say hi?"

Now there's a thought. Maybe you could share your tuna fish with them.

"Naw. That's okay."

"*Gaa*-ry! You can't stay by yourself all the time."

Why not? It works for me.

"You should mingle with kids your own age."

Should, should, should...

I stay put and silent, losing myself in the action, occasionally glancing over to my former posse.

Lizzy notices that I'm watching her. She turns and spots me hiding behind my mother and throws a hearty wave. I pretend not to see her.

It didn't work. Oh, no. Here they come. Half the crew gets up and meanders their way through a packed crowd. Crap! Crap! Crap! I'm not prepared for this again. I think I'm going to wet my pants. I need to quit sucking the water fountain dry to satisfy my hunger.

A roar erupts within the home bleachers. Someone shouts, "Way to go, Rick! What a play!" I turn to see a swarm of tall, sweaty guys bopping up and down around my brother. He must have—

"Oh, hi, everyone!" I exclaim.

We do this again...

"Hey, Gary. How's it going?"

"Hi, buddy. It's good to see you."

"Whazzzup?"

"So they let you out of solitary, huh?"

One of the boys reminds me of Mark Ponchkin, the grade school bully who used me as garden rake.

You're such a cream puff.

Would you please quit reminding me?

They do some minor interrogation as to my presence here this evening. To avoid having them invite me somewhere after the game, I inform them I'm out on pass and need to go back to the hospital immediately after the game. They hover for a while and tell me they miss me.

How touching. I think I feel a sniffle coming on.

Shut up!

So shoot me.

My body feels like it just fell into a campfire, and I want to get out fast. Seconds later, the group—all except Lizzy—shuffles to the concession stand, after which they return to their original bleacher section with enough sugar to rocket a dozen three-year-olds to the high-wired level for a month. How can they eat all that stuff and still have bodies like they do? Don't they ever feel guilty? I wish I could do that.

Lizzy nestles herself between Mom and me. "It's good to see you again, Gary."

"Yeah, you, too."

"You know, Gary, I really admire your courage. It must be hard to come back here and face everyone." Her knee bumps mine. My stomach does a somersault.

"Thanks. It's nothing, really."

We sit in silence, watching the game. I have no clue what to say to her. I love being around girls, but they make me feel uncomfortable, like the times I've had to give a speech in front of class.

"What's it like up there?"

I turn to look at her momentarily, then back to watching the game. "Well, it's not a picnic, but it's alright. The people are really nice, and it's helped me so far."

She squirms and looks at her watch. "I better get going. It's great to see you again, Gary. Maybe we'll talk again soon."

She gets up and works her way back through the bleachers to meet up with Gordon Zietminster, her boyfriend.

Nice going, jerk. You ruined someone else's evening. Girls and you just don't mix.

I sigh, regretting ever opening my mouth. I'm such a clod with girls.

Another cheer blasts around me, taking my mind off the stress. The game is exciting. It goes down to the last minute, with my brother sinking the last shot with ten seconds left on the clock. This puts the team ahead for good, causing a monstrous uproar from the packed crowd. My folks and I wander down onto the court to congratulate Rick on yet another brilliant game. What's he going to think of my being here? Will I disgrace him in front of his friends? He has no clue I came tonight. I stay hidden behind Dad. Rick is mixed in among a mob of well-wishers. Suddenly, his proud eyes meet my bony exterior, but only for a second. I better make the first move and get it over with.

"Nice game, bro."

Rick's face changes, from hyperexhilarated to surprised and stony, but only for a split second. Then it's on to indulge in the surrounding fanfare. Maybe he didn't see me.

Yes he did. He's ashamed to call you his brother.

How do you know that?

Looks speak more than words.

I'm beginning to question that philosophy.

I am so proud of my brother. He's so talented, funny, popular, and smart. I use to rove those hills at one time.

I sigh. I can't wait to return to the hospital. We slowly amble our way back to the car. I take one bite of my apple and a few crumbs of my sandwich. I pitch the rest into a nearby bush.

At least you won't have to lie if staff asks you if you ate your snack.

We discuss my brother's game for a few minutes, until my dad gets this far-out idea.

"How about we go for ice cream?"

"Ooooh, now that sounds like a good idea," says Mom, rubbing her hands together. "Where do you want to go, Gary?"

Give an excuse.

"The staff said I have to get back home as soon as the game ended."

"Home!" exclaims Mom, whirling her head around at me so fast I thought she broke her neck.

"Oh, uh, I mean the hospital."

"That place in not your home, Gary! Your home is with us! I can't believe you like it up there so..."

I feel like a two-year-old before being sentenced to a time out. Dad stays quiet and keeps driving. Icy silence infiltrates the car.

You are such a miserable, pathetic, wretch. How dare you upset your mother like that?

Dad passes by the Dairy Duck.

At least I don't have to suffer through eating ice cream.

"You know, Gary," says Mom, "other kids would jump at the chance to get ice cream right now."

Yeah, I know. I've heard that song before.

Your parents do so much for you.

Get off my back.

You know, Gary...

Shut. Up.

You're worthless.

We pull up in front of the emergency-room entrance. I get out of the car and say good-bye to my folks as if I'm going to a friend's house for dinner. My parents wish me a pleasant evening with a disappointed look under their brows. I hate that look. It's death to me.

They're ashamed to have you as a son.

They drive away as I enter the emergency entrance and greet familiar personnel as I do every time I come back from a pass.

It feels good to be home again.

CHAPTER TWENTY

D-DAY

I sense a volcano beginning to bubble under my chest at breakfast the next morning. I look down at my tray. Now what? They forgot to send two-percent milk up on my tray this morning, and I have two bowls of cereal to eat. What the heck is going on in that stupid hospital kitchen?

Whoa, calm down, tiger.

Leave me alone, just for once, *please*!

No can do.

I inform Hadie of the cafeteria blunder. She asks Atalanta to check the kitchenette for another carton of milk—she doesn't want to take her eyes off me. Have I slipped up somewhere hiding food? Did they find those sausages in my napkin? Are they onto my little schemes?

All that's found in the fridge is chocolate milk.

"I can send down for another carton of two percent." *Sniff.*

By the time they get back up here, breakfast time will be over and I don't want to be late for group therapy. *Sniff.* Oh, great! Now she's got me doing it.

"No, that's okay. I'll just use the chocolate milk."

"It's no problem to get another carton, Gary."

"No, really," I reply with a hint of sarcasm. "I'll go with the chocolate milk, please."

"Are you sure?" *Sniff.*

"Yes, really. I've had it before. It tastes like Cocoa Crunchies."

Another lie. This is becoming second nature to you.

Believe it or not, this actually tastes great. It reminds me of a rich-tasting dessert without the high fat, although I will have to exchange the extra calories with something else. From then on, I mark only chocolate milk for breakfast. I guess change isn't always bad.

I head into the group room after meal observation. We have a packed house this morning, twenty patients strong. Arty asks me if I would like to begin group with the opening monologue of confidentiality and group expectations. I like this. It gets me feeling important.

Interestingly, there is no one remotely close to my age on the unit at this time. I am the baby. The older generation looks at me like a grandchild. It's easy to communicate with this crowd. The expectation to perform isn't there. It's like they care, but they really don't care. My hypothesis is that they've already lived most of life and mellowed out, not sweating the small stuff anymore. They accept me for who I am and support me no matter what comes out of my mouth. What a refreshing attitude. I wish it were mine.

It ain't gonna happen.

Doreen takes the chair opposite Arty as usual. Something particularly eerie emanates over the flock this morning. Of course, I've felt this creepiness for the last couple of weeks, almost on a daily basis. I've dodged many a bullet lately from Arty's perplexing weaponry to lure self-disclosure from unsuspecting groupies. It's become a game of sorts between him and me—him wanting me to divulge the inner fuses of my circuitry, and me avoiding it like the flu. So far, I've gone undaunted in my mission of keeping others at arm's length. I don't care to talk about me, and I have no plans for today to be different.

The first few minutes are silent. I take a quick inventory as to who's fallen victim to Arty's devices this week. I can see only a couple of patients who haven't spoken much—one is John, an alcoholic, and the other is Pat, a suicidal woman who was admitted late last night for attempting to take her life by straddling her Pinto over train tracks.

Of course, if you owned a Pinto, wouldn't you be desperate, too?

You know, that's not funny at all. This is a hurting human being we're talking about.

Boo hoo.

Fortunately, curious neighbors called 911 before a train caught up with tragedy.

Then there's me, intractable and resolute in my stance, never bowing to the control of anyone else.

Except me.

I will not be defeated.

Think again. I'm in charge.

I'm strongly debating that lately.

Arty stares at me like something is on his mind. My eyes reflexively scamper to take refuge among the many chair legs below. Every few moments I come up for air to check on Arty's status. He continues to stare at me.

C'mon, pick on Pat. She's got fresh fodder for the mill.

Doreen picks up on Arty's vibes and looks at me, too.

Oh, great. Now I have both of them to contend with again.

It's nothing you haven't dealt with before. No problem.

I simply talk about some basic personal material that appears to be of a rather sensitive nature to satisfy their cravings and slowly manipulate the conversation away from me. It works like a charm. All of a sudden, out of nowhere, I get hit with a sneak attack from an unsuspecting foe—of all people, Pat.

"Gary, I understand you've been here for a long time now and have barely said a word about anything. I'm wondering what's up with that."

What the—? You're new. You haven't earned the right to make that observation yet. My temperature heats up. I feel my cheeks blushing. Arty and Doreen look at each other in surprise, then back to me to observe how I plan to worm my way out of this one.

"I've been doing well," I say, trying dreadfully hard to maintain a smile. "I really don't have anything to talk about that's different from before."

The group stares blankly.

"Really," I say. "I'm being honest. I've been doing very well lately. My passes are going well. My weight is up. Discharge should be right around the corner. I'm a happy camper."

The group keeps staring.

They probably have an alliance against you.

Arty looks bored. He leans forward with his chin propped up in his hand while resting his arm on the chair. Doreen does the same. They look like twins.

"Pat has a good question," says Arty.

Doreen gives a little nod. "I'm curious as to what the answer is going to be."

Defend yourself.

"Like I said before, I don't know what else to say. I'm doing well."

I continue dribbling on about how effective I believe therapy has been for me. Arty doesn't seem to be buying my sales pitch, so I keep yapping away about how I believe I've identified with patients over the weeks.

There, that ought to appease his appetite.

"So how long is it going to be?" asks Arty.

Wait a minute. Something is backfiring.

"What do you mean? What's wrong?" I gulp. "Did I say anything was wrong?"

He gives Doreen a dubious look while placing his hand on his chest, then looks back at me. He awaits a response. I buckle my lip. I know my cheeks are red—I feel like I'm overheating.

Emergency! Emergency! Don't let them get the best of you!

"You can't stay on Unit 13 forever you know," continues Arty.

"I know."

"What are you afraid of?" asks Doreen.

"What do you mean?"

Doreen shakes her head and chuckles. "Boy, he's good, isn't he, Arty?"

Arty bows his chin without taking his eyes off me.

It's getting worse. Battle stations!

I sneak a peek at the clock and curse in my head.

"There's plenty of time left, Gary. You've got all of group time if you want it," Arty says.

He's as sharp as ever this morning. I think he must know my every thought, my every manipulative move. I squirm and churn in my chair.

How are you going to get out of this?

Me? Aren't you going to help me?

No answer.

A volcano seethes. I feel it bubbling. My stomach feels like someone squirted a thousand lemons inside it.

"I don't know what to say," I say defensively, now feeling extremely alone.

"Did I say you *had* to say anything?" asks Arty, resting his hand upon his chest once again.

IT? IT? Where are you? Help me!

No answer.

"Well, you said you wanted me to talk about what's going on inside me. I believe I've done that."

"That's great, Gary," says Arty. "I'm glad you can open up to us."

I sense sarcasm. Silence hits the floor once again. His stare stubbornly refuses to move on to someone else. He wants me to do something, but what? I've shared all I know about what's going on inside me. I don't get it.

Don't go there.

Whew! There you are. What do you mean, "Don't go there"?

Another patient speaks up, someone whose name I can't seem to remember. "I've been up here a week now and I haven't heard more than a peep from you. I guess I've been wondering what you've been thinking of my situation."

The others murmur in agreement.

Your situation? You want my opinion?

"Well, uh..." This is bizarre.

The hush increasingly spreads through the room like smoke. All eyes are glued on me.

I hate this. Hate it. Hate it. Hate it.

"I would think being male with an eating disorder is rather difficult, being that most are women and all," comments Pat.

Good. This has possibilities of escape.

Don't go there!

What are you talking about?

"Yeah, sometimes," I say, my voice beginning to crack. "I mean, I—I really don't know of any other male who suffers—"

"What's going on inside you right now?" Arty interjects.

I gulp. "What do you mean?"

This response is now officially number six on my list of top responses.

"What I observe with you is that you talk a good game but lack emotional expression. You do a lot of talking about feelings but don't actually feel them."

"I show feelings. I'm frustrated right now and I'm showing you that."

"Frustration can be a rather hazy emotion," explains Arty. His stare remains fixed on me.

"What do you mean?"

"You're evading the issue."

Do. Not. Go. There.

What are you talking about?

Fermenting emotion transforms to simmering—

Oh, no! You're losing it!

—then to churning, then to boiling.

They're all against you! Stand firm! Don't let them C-O-N-T-R-O-L you!

Find a happy place, find a happy place, find a happy place...

Sweltering heat rises from deep within my chest. It creeps its way up my esophagus and settles in my sinus cavity, causing a torrent of wetness that blurs my vision. I am extremely warm and begin to shake with nervous tension. All eyes are fixed on me. Arty stares, and stares, and stares. I'm having a hard time breathing normally.

Arty whispers, "What's going on inside you right now, Gary?"

No response, just shaking.

"It's okay, Gary. Let it come. Let it come."

A creepy stillness slithers its tentacles around my throat. I attempt to escape the suffocating moment by focusing on the knocking heating vents in the background, but to no avail.

IT? Where are you? Come back. Help me, *please*!

Nothing.

The tension is too overwhelming, and then...

A tender whimper leaks from the side of my mouth. Teardrops begin trickling down my cheeks and onto my lips. I'm surprised at their taste—a bitter, sharp, salty flavor. My snivel turns to a moan, turning my rusted, spider web–clustered emotional crank to a full-blown sob.

NOOOOOOOOOOOOOOOO! YOU'RE GOING TO PAY FOR THIS, YOU WIMP! YOU'RE GOING TO HATE THIS. THIS IS GOING TO FEEL—

Absolutely wonderful!

My lament is uncontrollable. Forget speaking. This abrupt emotional outburst is so foreign to me, but it feels refreshing. Doreen has gotten out of her chair to comfort me. She kneels at my side. Emotional pus begins to ooze from my lips.

"I—I—I, h-h-hate th-th-this. I—I—I d-don't w-w-want this any m-m-more. I w-w-wish someone c-c-could take it all aw-w-way. Th-the v-voice in m-m-my head just d-d-doesn't stop. Well, i-it's not a r-r-r-real voice, like I'm c-c-c-crazy. M-more like my c-c-c-conscience. It just w-w-won't leave. I- don't know w-w-what to do to get rid of it..."

I cry and cry and cry and cry and cry and cry. IT is swept away in a monstrous tidal wave of ancient, stale, decomposed, fermented feelings. It goes on for many minutes. I become aware of a soothing revitalizing sensation slowly beginning to take shape. An incredible weight gradually falls away from my shoulders. It feels so good—so, so good. Gradually, speaking becomes an option again.

"I feel so...so...I don't know...*weird* to cry like this."

"There's no reason for you to be embarrassed," Arty reminds me. "Crying is a wonderful healing tool."

Others get up one by one to pat me on the back. My grief continues. The wailing has been downgraded to a shallow sniffle. The cat is out of the bag.

The dark drapes of inhibition have been torn down from a window that opens into all that is sincere within my soul.

"I hate myself," I blurt roughly, "but I don't want to hate myself. For the longest time I've lived in fear of the unknown, of wondering what people would think of me if I just acted like myself. I don't know who that person is. I try to incorporate the characteristics I like from other people into my personality, but it doesn't last. I'm sick of it." Doreen hands me a tissue.

I feel like I'm attached to some villainous creature that brainwashes me into thinking I'll be happy being someone I'm not. I'm not allowed permission to be free unless I follow strict, impossible-to-live-up-to standards. I'm damned if I do and I'm damned if I don't.

"I just can't win," I continue. "Yet, I always seem to come back to...to... to..." I sit and ponder for a moment, wiping more tears with another tissue Doreen hands me. I shift in my chair, unable to get comfortable all of a sudden.

"To what?" asks Arty.

I have to think hard about that.

"To what, Gary?"

"I wish I knew. Something I... Well, I don't know... Something I don't want to talk about I guess. At least that's what these books Greta gave me seem to tell me, something unconscious."

"You mean something in your subconscious?" asks Arty.

"Yeah, I guess."

"Who are you?" asks Arty. "What do you stand for? What do you believe in?"

"I don't know," I say. "I've never really thought about it."

"How come?

A snivel or two still lingers in my voice as I acutely ponder questions I've rarely, if ever, spent time with. To me, there are simply too many questions that require too much work to answer. It's all so confusing, especially when I don't have my own identity to stand on.

"There's always time to start," says Arty.

I sit up straight, tissues balled in my hands. "So what do I do?"

"Maybe grab a piece of paper and a pen, find a quiet corner, and do some deep soul searching," Arty offers. "Begin journaling your heart out. Throw any inhibitions to the wind—no pressure, no influence from others, no time limit. Cut the cord holding you fast to that voice you mentioned."

It sounds so easy to you, but you're not me.

Arty continues, his clenched fist punching the air. "You have the *choice*. You have the *power*. You decide your course. There's a saying that goes 'You can't control the wind, but you can adjust your sails.' Focus on your sails, and use the wind to your advantage. But you have to first untie the boat and get out on the water."

My expectations of people, of this group anyway, have been proven wrong. They're not laughing at me. There are no funny looks or crude sarcasm to be found. They're just a bunch of ordinary, everyday people supporting each other through many of life's unfair treatments. We're on equal turf up here, no matter what the age difference. We listen. We share pain and heartache. We ask questions. We empathize without feeling sorry for each other. We find the support to heal and gather strength to go on.

"It's about time you came out of your shell," says Doreen, messing up my hair. "We knew you were in there somewhere."

I smile. I knew it. She and Arty set me up the whole time. My respect and trust for them has increased four-fold.

The clock runs out for today. We head up the corridor to lunch. Arty puts his arm around my shoulder and pulls me in close. "You did good today, Gary."

I did, didn't I?

Confidence gives me a gentle pinch. I listen hard. IT is nonexistent.

My villain—slain?

CHAPTER TWENTY-ONE

ILLUSION THEORIES FOR ALL OCCASIONS

They are pumping 3,200 calories a day into my body now. Well, it's more like 2,800; 400 are being extinguished through underground (undertable) and underpants methods. I'm beginning to think they're bulking me up for a tryout with the Green Bay Packers' offensive line. Do they know what they're doing? If I eat the calories I'm packing in napkins and down my pants, logic says it's just a matter of time before my arms bloat up like stuffed kielbasa.

My workout classes, group excursions around hospital grounds, and walks downtown aren't cutting it anymore. My stomach is stretching and I don't feel as bloated after meals. Dr. Buckmier says my weight is still way below normal limits for someone my age and size, but at a livable stage. The dreaded "d" word (discharge) is scheduled for tomorrow. From the way I see it, either they're finally getting sick of me, or my parents' credit card has hit its limit.

Since yesterday's group therapy encounter, my appetite for self-actualization has been satisfied enough to tied me over for a while. I need to slow down. Change still remains as difficult as ever, but I truly want to live a different life. Of course, in order for that to happen, I'm going to have to start talking about my feelings more in group and maybe even consider Arty's suggestion of getting some ideas down on paper about who I am, what I like and don't like, career interests, and any other thoughts that don't involve IT. On the other hand, what if I don't like being healthy and find out that my best friend is gone, never to return? How is it going to feel? Will it be manageable? Will people give a hoot what I think they're thinking of me? If I believe they're thinking what I think they're thinking, I think I want to keep thinking how I think they're thinking because what I'm thinking are thoughts I can think and not be worried about what I think they think they're thinking...I think. I'm so confused.

Bob has his own mind-boggling theory: "You know, Gary, you think too much."

"Yeah, I know."

What am I talking about? I haven't the foggiest idea what he's talking about. "On second thought," I admit, "what do you mean exactly?"

Bob chuckles, his big belly jiggling up and down under his sweater like a paint mixer. "Lighten up. Go with the flow. Don't analyze everything to death. Use your gut instincts more. Don't take so much time to make some decisions. Just pick something, go with it, and see what happens. Live the moments, learn from them, and move on. Be spontaneous."

"But I'm afraid I'll make the wrong decisions."

"Such as?"

"Well, for one thing, I'm afraid if I pick the wrong foods, my stomach will feel stuffed and heavy, like a damp sponge."

"I don't want to sound too insensitive, but what's the big deal if it does feel a little full and heavy? God didn't design your body to just swell right up after a Thanksgiving splurge every now and then. Your body doesn't process food that way. Gaining weight is a gradual thing, and depends upon genetics and activity level, not just caloric intake."

"But I hate that fat feeling after I eat."

"Well, it's not about food, Gary. You know that," Bob says. "Plus, how your body feels is deceiving at times, especially when you've starved it for so long. Until you continue feeding it the proper calories it needs, it's going to continue feeling all out of whack. But the main thing is dealing with the underlying issues. The food thing falls in place over time."

"Yeah, I guess so," I say, sighing.

"Keep in mind that, up here, you're on a precise number of calories that a boy your age should be eating to simply maintain weight. Look at how long it's taken you to gain weight up here. Plus, your activity level has been severely limited while you've more than quadrupled your caloric intake compared to what you were eating at home," he points out. "How do you think this IT character you speak of matches up with the facts?"

I shrug my shoulders.

"If you're into comparisons so much, it's probably wise to spend more time with comparing your irrational messages with the facts of reality at hand. Stay here. I'll be right back."

Bob disappears into the corridor and returns with a piece of paper with a couple of four-sided shapes traced on it. The top shape is larger than the bottom one. Three of the sides on each shape are colored blue, and the bottom side of each is red.

"Take a look at the red lines," says Bob, holding up the picture. "Which one is longer?"

Immediately I choose the top red line. It's quite obvious. Bob hands me a ruler to check my answer—the incorrect one.

I'm amazed. My first impression told me for sure it was the top red line. "What? How can that be?"

"Have you ever heard of an optical illusion?"

"Mind tricks, right?"

"Kind of. They're brain tricks." Bob rubs his chin, turning the pictures this way and that. "Let me see, how do I explain this to you... When you look at two objects such as these, your eyes and brain work together to identify what they are. In this case, all your eyes see are lines. Your brain tells your eyes that they are straight, blue, red, square shaped, whatever. When your brain interprets a common figure over and over the same way, it gets used to interpreting it that same way, almost like your brain's on automatic pilot. For instance, when you see a large object next to a smaller one," he situates the pictures directly next to one another, "it usually means that the larger object has longer sides, and in most cases it does. But, in this picture, the larger shape has a shorter bottom side. Your brain was tricked."

I study the pictures closely, trying to put two and two together. "So, how does this apply to me?"

"We live in a harsh, image-worshiping society. We're constantly inundated with images of perfectly chiseled bodies in popular magazines, and skinny, doctored-up, pimple-free television characters."

My thoughts stray to the countless hours I spend paging through *Sports Illustrated*.

Bob continues, "Pretty soon, your brain starts to think that this is normal. But it's not. You stand in front of a mirror and chastise yourself for being too fat or not showing enough rippled muscles because you've been programmed to think this is normal from what the media throws at you."

"You mean these glossy pictures of super athletes aren't real?"

"No, they're real," says Bob, "but they're mainly of people who make a living with their bodies. They're a very small portion of our population, probably less than one percent. Magazines need to make money, so they snap shots meant to grab your attention. You, in turn, filter these pictures through your eating disorder mindset, and messages of what you should look like get twisted. They can turn in to somewhat of an illusion to you, just like this example I showed you. You're being duped by the boob tube for the sake of their popular ratings and money."

"But it's so hard. Changing is so much work."

"Yes, I can't even imagine how difficult this must be for you. You are dealing with a lifetime of these twisted ideas. You're setting yourself up for failure if you expect them to disappear in a day or two. It's going to take lots of patient, persistent hard work to fight them off. They might never leave."

"Don't say that," I say, jokingly making a cross with my fingers, as if fending off a vampire.

Bob laughs. "I didn't mean it that way. But you will get better at reducing the power of these distorted messages. You might not believe this yet, but you really do have the power to set the course for how fast your recovery takes place. You can't control all of what happens to you, but you can control what you think about it, and that makes all the difference."

"Easier said than done."

"Of course. Much of life isn't black or white, it's gray. Keep in mind that each of us is different and what works for one person might be a flop for another. It takes time, practice, and patience," Bob says, "but there's a basic framework that has proven to be effective over time with eating disorders and that's the protocol you're on now. We make mistakes of course, but we're willing to take risks for the sake of learning and your health. We would never do anything to intentionally make things worse for you up here."

A gentle whisper deep down, something entirely different from IT, says he's right.

I suddenly hear a long-winded sniff out in the corridor. There's a knock at the door.

"Excuse me, Bob," says Hadie. *Sniff.* "Gary has a visitor waiting for him in the sunroom." *Sniff.*

"Sounds good," says Bob, playfully punching my shoulder. "Enough of this talking stuff. Enjoy your visitor."

I walk to the front desk as Bob wanders away in the opposite direction. I wonder who my visitor is. I'm not expecting my parents until—

"Chandra!" I exclaim.

"Hey there, stranger," says Chandra. She looks fantastic—cheery smile, outfitted in designer jeans and matching sweater, so full in the face looking all healthy and healed. "It's been, like... forever—or maybe more like a few weeks." She gives me a hug.

Hadie winks at me before shutting the door, leaving Chandra and me alone. My body language reads "cool tomcat," but I'm a hooting and cackling hyena inside.

"It's so good to see you again," I say. She smells drop-dead good.

"You, too." We pull up chairs facing each other. "So how's life been treatin' ya' in this circus?"

"Pretty good," I say. "I'm being discharged tomorrow." Saying these words turns the lining of my stomach into paste.

"Really? Good for you, Gary," she says, grinning. "I'm so happy for you. Another defeat for the dark side."

"Yeah," I reply, eyes gazing longingly at her cheery face.

"How'd the staff treat you? Did Hormonal Hitler make you form swastikas with your mashed potatoes?

"Who?" I ask, looking puzzled.

Chandra looks confused, too, as if I'm kidding. "Atalanta, of course."

"Oh, yeah," I say, laughing, while watching Chandra shake her head. "Well, no, not this week."

We spend the next ten minutes chewing the fat and getting reacquainted.

Chandra is back in training for gymnastics and hoping to spring a position on the national team for next year. Her eating disorders seem to have never existed. Since she left the unit with a long face, her high spirits surprise me. What a change. I hope to wear her shoes.

Chandra explains, "I'm finished, Gary. I'm really finished—with my eating disorders that is. I'm sick of them. I don't need them anymore. Life suddenly seems more interesting. Ariel—one of the third-shift nurses—recommended that I cap off my transition away from the dark side with some type of good-bye ceremony—a good-bye to my old self, my old tools of the trade, my old patterns of thinking and behaving, my IT voice—"

Your what?

"—so we made an appointment to take a trip to the dump where there's this incinerator thing. I tossed everything down the chute—the clothes I used to wear, my worn out running shoes, the many buckets I used to hide vomit in, you know, stuff like that. It was awesome."

My mind simmers. "You know. I was wondering..." I stammer for a second or two, contemplating whether or not I should trespass these grounds, but I need to know. "You said something before about giving up a voice?"

"My stupid eating disorder. It's not really a voice or anything. It's more like my conscience, like that little devil on a person's shoulder. Ariel had me write a letter to this thing in my head, telling it to buzz off for good. And I quit calling it IT, too. Ariel told me the more attention I gave it, the more it would hound me. I learned it's not who I am anyway and doesn't need to be given a name. Before I tossed my letter down the chute with the rest of my junk, I tore it up into a zillion pieces." Chandra pretends to tear an imaginary piece of paper and throws it away like a baseball. "It looked like falling snow." Her face looks pleased, as if watching the tiny pieces of paper twitter away into oblivion, along with her mutinous eating disorder.

"Wow! So you haven't been bugged by IT—uh, your eating disorder—since?"

"Well, not really. These messages are still in the back of my brain, but I've learned to stomp them out with the new thoughts. Listening to this devil voice all the time was like... how do I explain this... Hold out your right leg as straight as you can."

"What?"

"Humor me, okay? Hold out your right leg—stiff like a board."

I follow her directions.

"Now, twirl your leg clockwise and, without changing the direction of your leg, try and draw the number six in the air with your right hand."

I can't do it. Each attempt at writing the number six with my finger ends up sending my leg circling in the opposite direction, no matter how hard I try to keep it from doing so. "How can this be?"

"I don't know," says Chandra, as I keep attempting the maneuver again—failing each time. "Ariel showed me. It has to do with the way the body is wired, or something like that. Anyhow, that's what I felt like when this eating disorder was in my life. I seemed to be fighting against something that I couldn't control, no matter how many times I tried. But these stupid tapes in my head kept tempting me with deals that couldn't be delivered, like telling me I could get better and finally be happy if I just got down to a certain weight, exercised enough, or binged and purged just one more time, so I kept right on battling. I was, like, incredibly stubborn and bullheaded."

"You? Chandra? Bullheaded?"

Chandra turns pink and slaps my arm hard. "Shut up, will you?"

"Sorry," I say, chuckling. "Go on."

"Well, I got so bad that I became almost numb to any help given to me. It was as if recovery was reserved for other people, and it was only a dream for me. But then it just got to the point where it wasn't worth it anymore."

"So what caused your change of heart?"

"I don't know. Mainly talking about it, I guess. It seemed like the more I talked about how I was feeling with everything, the less powerful my little devil got—like I pulled a plug or something. Journaling really helped, too. You should try it sometime."

There's a tap on the door before it cracks open to Hadie, "Excuse me, kids," *sniff,* "but Chandra, your father is here. I'm afraid you're going to have to wrap it up." *Sniff.*

"Crap," says Chandra, kicking my chair leg. "Yeah, yeah, be right there."

We get up to leave and say parting words. I feel angry that I can't visit with Chandra any longer.

"Well, good-bye, Gary." She grabs and squeezes me in a tight hug.

I'm hoping against all odds she'll say yes to this next inquiry. "We'll write and call, right?"

She lets me free, clears her throat, and makes as if something just flew into her eye. "Uh...sure, though I'll be pretty busy."

"Is there anything wrong?"

"No, not really," she says, not wanting to meet my eyes. "It's just, well... I've been seeing this guy for a while. He's a gymnast and..."

I knew it. My heart drops into the toilet and swirls down the drain.

"Say no more," I reply happily, trying not to end on a sour note. "He's one lucky guy."

Chandra smiles. "Don't worry, Gary. A guy like you isn't going to last long as a bachelor. Believe me."

Hadie gives a fake cough, "Excuse me again, Chandra," *sniff*, "but—"

"Fine, I'm coming!" Chandra snaps, making her way to the door. "Take care, Gary."

"You too."

She pauses at the door and gives me one last smile. "You're going to conquer this thing, Gary. I can feel it. You're more than just a stupid old eating disorder."

I want to believe her with everything that's in me. I guess our little visit is living proof that recovery is possible. Now if I could just put Chandra's brain into my own skull, life would be so much easier.

CHAPTER TWENTY-TWO

THE LETTER

My bags are packed, my bed is made, and Dr. Buckmier has analyzed me for the last time. It's amazing how much junk a person accumulates during a hospital stay. The visitors' waiting room by the front desk houses three large steel push carts of paraphernalia ready to make the trip to our car in the parking lot. I've got cards from dozens of well-wishers, balloons strapped to all ends of the carts, flowers, baby plastic water pitchers, pillows, clothes, and probably most of the knickknacks from the hospital gift shop. I should receive some type of frequent buyer discount for cleaning out their inventory.

Mom is at the front desk with Wal-Mart and Greta, going over discharge papers.

I roam the unit one last time to make sure I didn't leave anything behind. I'm going to miss this place. It was my home away from home for sixty-five days. My Chair is already occupied by a rookie patient admitted this morning. I find myself wanting to shoo him away so I can sit in it one last time. That would be rude.

The chair next to it, the one Chandra usually sat in, is empty. I'm going to miss her.

I find none of my possessions lying idly around the unit, so I make my way toward the front desk. Arty and Greta are now conversing with Mom. She seems flustered, as if debating with Arty on some hot issue. Arty shakes her head with an expression of complacency. This is a side of my mother I rarely see: debating with someone. She could usually model for the cover of *Smooth Sailing Weekly*. As I approach the desk, all go quiet. Facial expressions take a 180-degree turn from being distraught.

"Well, are you ready, Gary?" Mom asks brightly.

I nod my head. Arty gives me a firm handshake and wishes me the best of luck. Greta and Wal-Mart follow suit. Jezi zips down the corridor from the O.T. room to do the same, then zips back. Wide smiles ripple across everyone's faces. Mom looks disturbed. Something is wrong. She's on the verge of tears—I know that look. She forces a half smile. I look at my heavy suitcase and sigh, coaxing out an enabling moment.

"Here, Gary," says Mom, sensing my manufactured anguish, "I'll carry that for you."

Good. It worked.

"Ah, Gary," says Greta, peaking over her thick black, half-moon spectacles, "you can probably get that bag yourself, right?"

"Sure."

"Oh, okay. I'll push the cart," says Mom. Her voice sounds like a dark little rain cloud hovering over her head. "Thanks again, Greta, Arty, everyone, for everything."

Suddenly, Dad bounces onto the unit with boyish enthusiasm. "Gary, it's so good to see you," he raves, almost out of breath. He lays his big hand upon my shoulder, sparking a memory of when he practically strangled me like a boa constrictor while I did sit-ups during the morning of my admission. He turns toward the front desk, offering his hand to each staff person in turn, as if he's just completed a business deal. "Thank you, thank you, for all you've done for my son."

He turns to me excitedly, his eye popping. "Here," he says, handing me an envelope, "this arrived in the mail this morning. Take a look at who it's from!" His grin is so wide I think he needs two more cheeks to hold it. The return address says Kansas City Royals Baseball Organization. The staff awaits the news. I slice it open and read the letter aloud:

Dear Mr. Grahl,

We are pleased to inform you that you've been invited to participate in a private tryout camp at Milo Park in Milwaukee on Saturday, July 10th. Your coach has told us many good things about your baseball potential. Warm ups and drills will begin promptly at 11:00 a.m. An exhibition game will follow.

If you have any questions, please feel free to call me at 414-555-2968. We look forward to seeing you in action.

Sincerely,

Rocko Blitzke, Talent Scout

Kansas City Royals Baseball Organization

My body freezes, as if I'm being shocked with electricity. My thumb instinctively sniffs out the sharp, bottom corner of the letter, which is already being driven like a stake under my thumbnail. Force of habit.

"Well, congratulations, Gary!" exclaims Greta.

"Yes, well done," *sniff*, says Hadie.

After another round of handshakes, a middle-aged, bubbly nurse, someone I've only seen occasionally during the graveyard shift and that day my friends came to visit after prom, appears on the scene. She has short, spiky blonde hair and the energy of a young colt.

"Hello, everyone, I'm Ariel. I'll be escorting you down to the car."

We politely decline the offer but Greta insists—something about unit policy. We trod down the entrance corridor to Unit 13. Dad, still giddy over the news from Kansas City, treads ahead of me with Mom. Each pushes a cart. I straggle behind with Ariel.

"So," says Ariel, "how's it feel to be going home after being here for so long?"

Wow, you did your homework.

"Good. I can't wait."

She then hits me with a response from the blind side. "I know what's happening, Gary. It's okay to accept the struggle. Just pay attention to the real you."

I look at her quizzically. What do you mean you know what's happening? We've barely met. And what's this about accepting the real you?

I suddenly remember leaving a pair of shoes underneath a chair in the visitor's waiting room. "Ariel, I forgot a pair of my shoes. I'll be right back."

"No problem. We'll catch you at the elevator."

I scurry back to the front door of the unit and quietly step into the waiting room next to the nurse's station. Atalanta, Arty, Greta, and Wal-Mart talk and still mingle at the front desk. They fail to notice I've returned.

"What do you think, Arty?" says Atalanta.

"He's such a nice boy, too," says Wal-Mart. "Such a pity."

"The beast must follow its course to full term," says Greta. "Unfortunately, it's the only way in many cases."

A long pause curtails the conversation, which changes to idle talk about where they'll be doing lunch today. I idle my pace in an effort to eavesdrop for one last moment. My heart shocks by three disturbing words finally deriving from Arty that undoubtedly refer to me: "He'll be back."

Yes, I am.

PART II
THE NEW YOU

CHAPTER TWENTY-THREE

BACON ANYONE?

Mom thought a dose of manual labor over the summer—outside of my annual lawn mowing ceremony—would be good for my "problem." My folks subscribe to the adage that hard work builds character, and generous doses would purge any sort of ill-mannered behaviors that swayed from our family's straight and narrow.

Hence, my summer job title: Goalpost Molder. We the employees at P.J. Puck Enterprises are proud to call ourselves the nation's third leading manufacturer of premium quality ice-fishing equipment. Competition for ice-fishing equipment is fierce, and Mr. Puck has dollars on the brain.

My senior year starts in two months. I would die for a real summer vacation, but it's unwarranted; I haven't worked hard enough yet. Then again, senior year is the slack-off year. We'll see.

I toil away in a room called The Dungeon. It's a cool, musty corner of this craggy factory. My job comprises scooping molten lead into preformed casts that my coworkers maneuver to create depth finders. Lead is densely heavy, so it serves its purpose well to drop a fishing line to the bottom of a lake. Since the melting point of lead is 613 degrees Fahrenheit, I wear a fashionably bulky apron complemented by thick furry mitts and a tacky pair of safety glasses. I wouldn't wear this ensemble to a wedding, but it keeps me safe.

I set down a heavy iron tongs I use to handle hot scrap lead. Its weight puts a strain on my muscles, but I like what it does to my veins, causing them to stick out like lines on a road map.

You know, you deserve a Rambo scar. It's going to hurt, but oh well…

I deserve this. IT—that is, my eating disorder, doesn't need to remind me any longer. I can chastise myself just fine now. With losing all this weight since I was discharged (twenty-five pounds to be exact), "wasted failure" has become my middle name. My problem and I are now one, and I can't figure out what happened. It all seems like such a blur.

I snatch up a piece of red-hot scrap lead with the tongs and hold it up in front of my face. Heat waves make the air ripple. I route the tongs to my upper arm and slowly let the lead piece drag across my skin.

Sizzzzzzzzzzzzzzzzzzzle.

My stoic, numbed face barely winces. This feels so primitive, so emptying. Smoke from searing skin rises upward, pelting my nasal passages with a vile aroma. I ignore my nerves squealing in pain. My plan is to reduce the unfortunate segments of my arm to bacon. I'm a steer getting tagged by a blacksmith. Three inches of branding come to an end. I toss the scrap back into the pot. It liquefies instantly.

All those weeks of therapy on Unit 13, scattered to the wind. And to think your parents paid for it all. You should be ashamed of yourself.

I let the hot scrap metal skim across my arm once more—round two. The sizzling flesh reminds me of the splattering grease from Dad cooking sausages on Sunday morning. Six scars later, the torture is over. The burns are hardly noticeable. I'm disappointed.

Chatter. Chatter. Chatter. My coworkers materialize from around the corner, returning from lunch. Quick, sweatshirt back on. Ouch! I accidentally lean back on the crest of the melting pot. Bonus scar. One of the workers notices my surroundings.

"Aren't you just a tad warm in that sweatshirt?" asks a girl.

"For some reason all of a sudden, I feel a bit cold inside," I reply.

CHAPTER TWENTY-FOUR

AND THE AWARD FOR BEST ACTOR GOES TO...

Tryout day is finally here. In an effort to kill time on the way down, I make up a little ditty in my head on the way down to Milwaukee:

Rain, rain, stay right here,

It's a way to ditch my fear.

High school and college athletes alike,

Aspire for the dream since they were tykes.

Me? I can hardly imagine I'd make it,

My weight is too low, but it won't hurt to fake it.

What am I saying? Logic just doesn't fit,

I can barely get the ball to the first baseman's mitt.

A good performance is mandatory, I must achieve,

But from where did this attitude creep up my sleeve?

This car trip's a bear, I'm so angry at Dad,

For what though? He's been nothing but supportive and glad.

My heart is in prison doing twenty years to life,

For what is my crime that I endure this strife?

I work painfully hard, a nice guy to the core,

I don't deserve life to be one massive chore.

But a relentless lilt beckons, Aha, I must beg to differ,

Your sentence to gloom and doom should be stiffer.

You deserve nothing—freedom's cost is quite high,

Unconditional acceptance is only a lie.

Stick with my plan, there's security in every breath,

Choose wisely, my friend, or else you'll choose—

"You probably shouldn't have gotten up so early to work out this morning, Gary," says Dad, anxiously driving down Highway 41. This is a huge day for him. His son is "drinking coffee" with some big boys. "You'll need all the rest you can get."

Am I ever beat. My shoulders are sore. My knees are sore. My back is sore. My feet are aching. My sides hurt. I'm tired and cranky and voraciously hungry after yet another early morning militant workout. It's hard to imagine I'm back to square one, after all that hard work.

"I feel good, Dad," I say dryly. "I like to get my body warmed up. I'll be alright."

A good deal of the trip is spent with my head leaning on the window while making slight snoring noises, permitting my attention to roam and play in my head without disruption. I want to sniffle, but it will signal to Dad that I'm awake. I suffer through a runny nose. I should win an Academy Award today.

I hope Lizzy answers the letter I sent. I wrote to apologize for making her feel uncomfortable at my brother's basketball game. Although I must admit, I picked up a weird vibe from her. Something didn't seem right. On the other hand, I can't trust my gut about anything anyhow, so maybe it was nothing. If only I could borrow someone else's body and brain when I'm with girls, I'd be alright.

"You gotta eat more, Gary," says Dad. Exasperation over my pathetic performance last week in a baseball game causes him to squeeze the steering wheel until his knuckles go white. "I can't believe you had to get taken out of the game because you were too weak to throw the ball from third base to first base. Didn't you take your medication?"

No. I didn't think it would matter.

Zzzzzzzz. I'm such a good faker.

Dad and I finally pull into the parking lot of Milo Park, the baseball field of a local Milwaukee high school. The field looks impeccably tidy and groomed. A wide, fake yawn arouses me from my phony slumber.

"Good luck, Gary," says Dad, patting me on the back. "I'll be up in the stands watching the whole time."

Great. That'll help me play better.

I've also been informed by my coach that only two high school seniors were fortunate enough to get called to this tryout camp, of which I am one. Everyone else has either graduated or is fresh college meat.

Coaches and baseball scouts with stopwatches in hand fill the damp infield. They all hide behind Secret Service sunglasses and do a lot of pointing and ordering. I think it makes them feel important and intimidating. It works; my stomach churns something awful. I can't think. I dare not say a word. Everyone else acts like they know what they're supposed to be doing, like they've been around this block before. Somehow I get the feeling that more like me lurk among them.

The first drill is the sixty-yard dash. They line us up in two rows like kindergarteners. This promises to be embarrassing. I hate to admit it, but my speed has drastically diminished over the last couple of years. At least we'll be exercising and burning up calories.

Someone shouts "Go!" I lumber forward as fast as my hurting body will permit. Surprisingly, I begin parallel with my opponent, whose porky body happens to take the shape of Winnie the Pooh. He must be a catcher. Sheer exhaustion sets in thirty yards down the grassy path. Winnie wins by at least five lengths.

Why am I even here?

To infield practice we go. They order us to take the position we play most of the time. I plant myself at third base, sandwiched between two monstrous ogres glancing at each other like my presence must be some type of joke. They smell fear. Both are drooling over the chance to show each other up in front of the baseball hierarchy. Me? A dugout bench has my name on it. I'm a baby duck cruelly yanked from its mother. I need to get back to the unit.

It's time to lock myself in the magical land of imagination called Garyworld.

CHAPTER TWENTY-FIVE

AM I EVER GLAD TO SMELL YOU?

We interrupt this regularly scheduled program to bring you the following presentation...Well it's that time again, Charlie.

I think you're right, Johnny. It's time for everyone's favorite game show, Let's Be Somebody Else.

Who do we have for today's contestant, Charlie?

Well, Johnny, we have the ever-popular and all-time leader in days played here on Let's Be Somebody Else. So let's bang our hands together and give a warm welcome for your favorite and mine, Mr. Jim Gantner, all-star second baseman for the Milwaukee Brewers. Whoo! Whoo!

I walk like Jim, think like Jim, stand like Jim, and scratch like Jim. It's strict survival.

Whoa, Charlie. He's not looking up to snuff this morning, is he?

I'm afraid not, Johnny. He's usually right on the money. Maybe this level of nervous tension is too overpowering for the young lad. This is a big day for him you know, being squeezed under a heavy microscope and all, and I'm not referring to the baseball scouts.

I hear you loud and clear, Charlie. Do you think there is anything we can do for him, a quick shot of Ego Booster Elixir Extract maybe?

That's a negative, Johnny. This is a beast of his own creation.

All we can do is sit back and hope for the best, Charlie. Maybe he'll do better with this next attempt.

A grumpy hitting coach rockets another ground ball my way, and it happens to find the only torn lip of grass on the field. It pelts me square in the sternum and sends me sprawling back onto my hind quarters. I've been hit by a truck. Scrambling to gain composure, I fetch the ball bouncing errantly at my feet—ignoring the fiery burn in my chest—and fire it as hard as I can to the second baseman. My arm screams in agony. I failed to warm up. Asking anyone if they wanted to play catch was too frightening.

Within seconds, a third ground ball finds its way into my glove on a lucky short hop. I'm ready to really show them what my arm can do. Reaching back with every last ounce of strength, I let the ball fly across the infield and...dink-dink...plop. The ball softly jumps into the first baseman's mitt after two short hops. My arm cries out for mercy.

Actually, the ball didn't whiz across the field as hoped, Charlie, like the hurls of the two mammoths with him. And they barely exerted any effort. It's not looking good for our gold-hearted, faithful friend, is it?

No it's not, Johnny. I feel for the boy. If only he'd just, you know...

I couldn't agree with you more, Charlie.

Everyone on the field takes a seat. Excruciating pain throbs in my shoulder, worsened by the fact that there's no sensation in my arm from my elbow down. Amputation? I'd have an excuse to bypass this weird phase of my life. The coaches decide to play a nine-inning game and promise to get all of us playing time. Do we have to? I suffer through seven innings of fretful anticipation before I get the call to pinch hit, and then ordered to take third base once we reach three outs. I grab a bat and start taking practice swings like—

Charlie, is that what I think it is?

Yes, I think it is, Bob—the old switcheroo. It looks like... Ah, well, I believe it's all-star third baseman George Brett of the Kansas City Royals.

I dig my spikes into the batter's box like George and take a peek at the catcher, a massive head with a crew cut. The guy's built like a firehouse. I reckon he probably eats enough at one feeding to nourish a third-world country for a month. You mean I have to look like that to make it to the pros? Even the umpire looks like those brief glimpses of that Bigfoot character on the documentary *Mysterious Creature Sightings of the Woodlands*.

No sooner do I get myself situated in the box when I hear, "Strike one!"

Oh, my gosh!

The next pitch, a curve ball, comes buzzing past my waist, cutting an arch like a super mosquito and smacking into the mitt. "Strike two!"

My heart fretfully thumps in my chest. I step away from the plate to tap dirt from my spikes, stalling for time.

What the heck am I doing here?

My internal organs quiver violently, threatening to moisten my pants. I dig back into the batter's box, preparing to take some foul-tasting medicine. The pitcher winds up, the ball lets loose from his canon, I swing in desperation, and the end of my bat makes mediocre contact with an oncoming truck.

Ooooooooowwww!

Where did the remaining feeling in my arms go? The ball trickles up the middle past second base. Two pencil-like legs dart down to first base, to some extent unaware of the reality of what just happened.

A hit. I can't believe it, Charlie. The boy actually got a hit, a petty dribbler up the middle, nothing to write home about, but a hit nonetheless.

First base is a pedestal of honor. Every body part of me from my waist up is trembling in pain. My face is beaming. Since I'm sucking off the adrenaline hose at the moment, I decide to do something against my better judgment, something stupid. I attempt to steal second base.

Oh, no! Don't look, Johnny.

The gas gauge for my legs reads empty halfway down the base path. An awkward slide trips up the shortstop covering the base, causing the catcher's high throw to ricochet off the shortstop's head and carry into the outfield. The crabby third base coach turns three shades of scarlet. He shakes his head and scowls at me, looking as if a good disemboweling would do me good right about now.

The third out comes, and now I'm heading off the field with my eyes bonded to Mother Earth looking for grasshoppers. I can't look up. My blind navigation causes me to bump into a tree—no wait! It's a human, the grouchy third base coach. "Utterly ridiculous! What were you thinking, Grable?"

You're so unimpressive they can't even get your name right.

The poor boy is really getting chewed out now, Johnny. It's not a pretty sight.

I find my glove in the dugout. Laughing ensues from other players. They look at me and then snigger at each other. I didn't hear the joke.

For the next ten minutes, I engage in serious prayer at third base, hoping God is home. I try to make myself look good by futzing with my hat, just like Jim Gantner. My plan is to let the shortstop show off by picking up anything that's hit to this side of second base.

Shouting interrupts my plea to God. "Hey, third base. Get the bunt!" Darn it! I was playing too deep! My body stumbles toward home plate in a panic. I trip and fall, landing flat on my face, inches from the baseball.

Ooooooh! That hurt, Charlie. This is not looking good, such a sad moment for our heroic little friend.

Reality bites. I don't want to be Jim anymore. The heck with George. My frail frame lies still, with my nose squashed into freshly cut turf. For some reason, the fragrance of rich green earth comforts me. I am mortified and spent. I want to cry. I want to go home. I want my *Rambo* soundtrack and my Walkman, and I want to run forever. I want to beat my body into oblivion with torturous exercise.

What a wimp I am, nothing but a waste of space.

Calloused fingers wrap around my arm. "Are you okay, son?" All I can do is groan. "Freckenhammer! Grab a glove and get the heck out here. Take over for Grable."

Those are the best words I've heard all day. Two players help me hobble off the field while I turn in a stellar performance called "Gathering Sympathy from the Crowd by Faking a Twisted Ankle." At least I'm a good fibber, although it's nothing spectacular to write next to my name in the yearbook. It's over. I can relax.

And it looks like that's the ball game, Charlie—at least for now. He's back to being nobody again. What a sorry way to end a potentially star-studded production. The boy's got the tools. If he'd only employ the confidence to use them.

I agree, Johnny. I wholeheartedly agree.

Well, folks, it's been another wild ride on the imagination bandwagon. Join us next time for more exciting, frivolous fun on Let's Be Somebody Else. For your host, Johnny, this is your announcer, Charlie, saying good-bye and—

Excuse me, Charlie. Sorry to interrupt, but from the impression I'm getting up here in the press box... Now I'm only reading body language, of course... I'm wondering if the boy is forgetting one thing.

What's that, Johnny?

What's his father going to think?

Oh, nuts, Johnny. I forgot about him. And from the looks of our gallant friend, so did he.

CHAPTER TWENTY-SIX

ONE SHARP PACKAGE

Dad casually saunters over to the bleachers. I feel utterly humiliated. The cold steel bench feels like ice on my butt, and it's not from what my mom refers to as "no meat on my bones." He lays a hand on my back, asks if I'm okay, and smiles to congratulate me on my hit and stolen base. "You did good, Gary. You tried your best, that's all you can do." That's Dad language for telling me I sucked. He plays Mr. Diplomatic, but I know better. I've gravely disappointed him and probably embarrassed him as well. At least I'm two for two with something today. I want to be left alone.

Little else falls from Dad's lips as we make our way to the car. He takes a detour to the men's room. This lends me an opportunity to wander over to the fence behind home plate and watch a select number of players retake infield practice. I overheard someone mention that the standouts of the tryout camp would be re-tested for the possibility of signing minor league contracts. I expel a heavy sigh.

A dream, that's all this is—one big, bad dream. What was I thinking? I don't belong here. A dark emptiness fills my heart. I can't do this anymore. I just can't. There's nothing but heartache out here—having to deal with fickle people and their feelings. It's time to get away from all this pressure and return.

It's time to go home.

Excitement rushes through my veins. I'll begin preparations tonight.

My body assumes the same bogus sleeping position in the car going home as it did on the way down: slouched, head resting against the window with my cap blanketing my face, disturbed and troubled. Dad offers one of his best monologues on how adversity shapes a man's character and how success is not in never falling but in how many times a man gets back up and keeps going. He's been reading *The Peppy Farmer's Almanac* again. My sense is that his inspirational message is more for himself than me.

I am unstable.

My eyes begin to moisten with tears. I wipe, not permitting them to touch my cheek.

I am unbalanced.

Crying should be okay. Arty said so. It felt so good after I did it in group therapy.

I am so unimportant.

I never thought I'd say this, but I want to go back to Atalanta, to wise Greta, to ADHD Jezi, to Hadie and her obnoxious sniffing.

I am incapable.

Wow, you're doing it to yourself now. I don't even have to remind you.

Then again, nothing in me really seems to have genuinely changed, so why try anymore? In fact, I've gone backwards. It would just be throwing my parents' hard earned cash out the window.

Oh, God, why me?

I still feel the nagging sting from the hard ground ball that walloped me. Dad silently navigates the highway. His craggy face burns a blank expression through the windshield. Disappointment. He's witnessed a lot, this man: Korean war, four children (one of whom gives him nothing but unending grief), one wife, thirty-seven years of toil as a factory laborer for the same company with regular turnover of bad management, and just missed making it to the big leagues in baseball by the skin of his teeth. A broken leg and the war spoiled his dreams. Now it's my turn for a dream to evaporate.

He deserves a better son.

The rest of the evening is spent in a pit of pity. I make myself feel better by running my legs off before bedtime to my *Rambo* soundtrack. Sleep was minimal, as I brashly obsessed over my pitiful performance at the stupid tryout.

Early the next morning, a boxy brown truck wheezes to the curb. My spirits brighten. The UPS guy finally delivers my package after I've spent four long weeks waiting. It's a—well, I'd rather not tell. It's kind of, how shall I say, abnormal. Lately, I even find it more interesting than *Sports Illustrated*.

I intercept the driver halfway to our front door, quickly scribble my signature on his clipboard (looking up at the house to make sure Mom isn't peeking out the living room window), and dash through the kitchen on a mission to seclusion. The smells of dinner fill the air. It's onion meatloaf night—one of my favorites. Too bad I'm limited to only 200 calories this evening, and I won't be able to eat the chocolate cake I made earlier, either. It's my third dessert concoction this week. I love playing baker but never lick the spoon. Hidden calories pile up quickly. Instead, I watch others gorge on marble cake with cream cheese frosting, butterscotch torte, cinnamon coffee cake, and fresh apple pie while I nibble away on asparagus spears. People are so weak.

"What'cha got there, Gary?" asks Mom, suddenly appearing from the living room with a load of laundry.

Darn it. Not now. I have things to do. Scram. "More baseball cards," I mutter curtly, continuing the course to my room. I call it "lying on the run."

"Dinner will be ready in a couple of minutes, so don't go anywhere."

"Yes, Mom."

I kick the door shut with my foot and plunk down onto my bed, tearing open the package to reveal something I've been eyeing to buy since I saw the first *Rambo* movie. I thought it would only be a miniature replica of a movie prop especially designed for Sylvester Stallone's character, but

I'm pleasantly surprised that it's a life-sized—a genuine, stainless steel, fourteen-inch survival knife with built-in fishing line and saw blade.

Knock, knock, knock.

Aaaaaaah!

"Gary, can I come in?" asks Mom. "I have some laundry to put away."

I shove my package under my bed and snatch a *Sports Illustrated* off my trophy-covered dresser. "Yeah, okay."

She enters with a basket towering with neatly folded clothes. She quickly scans my room, curious to see what I'm up to no doubt.

"What'cha doing?" asks Mom, proceeding to sort clothes into drawers.

"Just reading."

Secret Agent Mom continues her laundry mission, but interrogates no further. She rarely does, especially about the goings on in my life, or any topic that might spur a small catfight. Feelings must stay smooth as glass.

"Dinner."

"Okay, be right there."

She exits my room, and, as usual, conveniently forgets to close my door. I click it shut, certain she does it purposely. Stupid games.

The table looks like a Dick's Big Boy Buffet. A large, steaming-hot pan of onion meatloaf glazed with lemon seasoning takes center court this evening, surrounded by a half dozen foil-wrapped baked potatoes the size of footballs, two heaping plates of sweet corn, three torpedo loaves of French bread smothered in creamery butter, a heaping mound of spinach salad with bacon vinaigrette dressing, and, of course, milk to drink. Gosh, Mom, it's only Dad, Rick, and me. Are the Harlem Globetrotters coming for dinner?

We barely finish the prayer and are already eased into our nightly dinner routine when I yawn for the fifth time in a matter of minutes. It's been another draining day. Paranoia sets in. I'm being assessed, I'm sure of it. They might be experimenting with me tonight.

I do a quick eye check. Right now, everyone's busy jockeying forks in the meatloaf pan. Dad begins his bantering about the crooks in top management at his work, and it's never an upbeat lecture—never. This takes us through most of the meal. Rick, who eats at the speed of sound, simply nods his head, tossing in a prefabricated opinion every now and then to let Mom and Dad see that he's still breathing. Mom jimmies a comment in about how many potatoes are left on the platter with an obvious glance at my plate, which is still scattered with food. Hint, hint. I continue to play table soccer with a crouton. It's less fattening.

While little brother plays decoy, I mentally tabulate exactly how many calories cover each plate on the table, mine being the lowest at all times. It must be that way.

"Here, Gary," says Mom, attempting the unthinkable. She sets her own small ear of sweet corn onto my plate, which rolls through my small mountain of ketchup. It even has one of her bite marks in it. "Eat that."

"I've got enough on my plate already, Mom."

Rick slaps Mom's hand for the tag team. "Just eat it, will you? It's just a stupid piece of corn."

Tempers have been touchy lately. My family knows very well that I've taken a turn for the worst, but it's been easier to simply ignore it and hope it goes away. This results in Family PMS. They keep trying to force me to eat; I doggedly refuse. The harder they push, the more irritated and bull headed I become, which in turn causes me to inflict all sorts of creative harm upon myself because I feel it's justified. They hate it when I get into this rut. It's a cycle I do over and over. I can hardly blame them for being ornery with me. I hate me, too.

I stick my spoon into my chocolate milk and stir, keeping to a sparse ten mixing revolutions with each hand instead of the usual fifty I do when I'm alone. It might stir up sensitivities this evening, but I must carry out my routine. Mom plops a hunk of salad onto my plate, even before my spoon switches hands. Not a good move on her part.

Without staring into her eyes, which I know are picking me apart, I scrape it back into the serving dishes. Weeping and gnashing teeth follows from Mom. I turn red and hide behind the defense of silence, reverting back to my private chocolate-milk-mixing ceremony.

Dad is fed up. He grabs my hand with ferocity, confiscates my spoon, and slams it across the table, all the while making entertaining contortions with his sun-wrinkled face.

"Hey!" I say, feeling horrendously ill at ease. "What's the deal?"

"What's the deal?" yells Dad. "What's the deeeeeeeeeeeeeeeeeal?"

So that's where Mom gets those long syllables.

"Don't you know that you don't have to listen to that awful eating disorder in your head? Don't let it get to you or it will destroy you. I'm not going to stand for this and watch my son slowly kill himself."

Action halts like someone hit the pause button on the remote. The only thing being chewed now is Dad's last few words.

Mom decides to bring the rocking boat back to balance. "Now, now, you two, let's take it easy. No sense fussing over stirred milk."

Rick snickers and nearly chokes to death on a chaw of meatloaf. Dad yelps like a bull being castrated.

In a last-ditch effort to calm rough seas and keep everyone off my back, I stuff an entire hard roll into my mouth. Everyone looks at me in disgust like I just sprung another head from my neck. Mom quickly redirects the conversation to choices of new floor covering for the living room. I make to wipe my mouth with my napkin, only to slyly spit out masticated food and ball it up without anyone being the wiser.

No sooner do I pat myself on the back for doing a brilliant job at being secretive when I make a devastating slip-up. Habit causes me to roll up my sweatshirt sleeve as I pretend to reach for another ear of corn. Mom's eyes turn as large as tennis balls. When I suddenly realize my disastrous mistake, it's too late.

"What on earth happened to you?" cries Mom, looking fixedly at my scarred arm.

"Oh, it's, uh..."

Oh, no! Think—quickly.

"It's just a little accident I had at work this summer."

I'm such a brainless— How could I forget—? I close my eyes and await the inevitable.

"Gaa-ry! Accident?"

"Yeah, I, uh..." Stalling is an art, similar to spreading food around on my plate. It needs a special touch, and timing is everything. Then an idea hits me. "Well, you see, when I was bending down to pick up my tongs that I knocked onto the floor, I accidentally bumped the table that had a pile of molten scrap lead on it. The pile came toppling down onto my arm."

Home run. Anxiety begins to subside. Mom and Dad's mental computers are slow on the uptake, still tabulating information.

"If the scrap fell on top of your arm, how did the scabs on the underside of your arm get there?" asks Rick. He quickly rams a forkful of potatoes into his mouth, looking all smarty-pants-like.

"I turned my shoulders back up like this—" I demonstrate a twisting maneuver with my upper body. "—toward the table and caught more scraps on their way down."

How can I continue to lie like this to my family? The guilt spigots are turned wide open, constricting my self-worth unmercifully. Dad says nothing and quietly grinds away at his corn like a cow, obviously on the verge of tears.

You've let him down again—big time.

"They're healing just fine," I say matter-of-factly, trying to make things sound better than they are. "I'll be fine."

"Sure you will," Mom says. "I can't believe you, Gary. If it's not one thing, it's another. Are you sure that's what happened?"

"Honest, that's what happened."

Somehow, guilt has shut off. I feel utterly empty and numb.

Mom's doubtful brow tells me she's not convinced, but she seems to be losing steam quickly. Methodical chewing of food is all I hear.

I take a deep breath, contemplating whether I should simply be open and straightforward, like I was in group therapy this past spring. It was uncomfortable, but the relief and self-confidence it brought were worth the effort. I could use a release right—

A shrill scream in my head suffocates the idea.

No. You will not. It's too difficult.

"But, Gary, what about all the counseling you've had?" asks Mom, now calmed a degree or two. "Surely, you've learned something."

"Yeah, I know. But for some reason, I can't seem to apply it to my life. It's like I never had counseling at all."

Clink. Dad drops his fork in mid-bite.

Whoops. Wrong move.

His waving hands and arms accidentally come down on the end of his fork, which is holding a chunk of meatloaf that now flies over the table and into the living room, smearing gooey shards of meat and ketchup over Mom's spotless carpeting.

"You mean I paid thousands of dollars for...for...for nothing?" yells Dad, nostrils flaring.

I pause, vigilant to watch where I trod. "Well, uh—yeah, I don't—"

"What did you say?" roars Dad.

"I said yes!"

I feel like one of Satan's little imps.

"Gaa-ry!" shrills Mom.

"You don't really mean that, do you?" says Dad.

"Well, I don't know. Maybe I do."

"I can't take it anymore... I'm going over to Billy's house... I'll be back at nine," says Rick. After one more swig of milk, he fumes outside to his beat-up Escort.

I forcefully stab my fork into a cold cob of corn with mouse-like bites taken out of it.

My folks continue conversing with each other as if I wasn't there. "So, Arty was right, then..." says Mom, looking at Dad for approval.

"I was praying that it wouldn't be true," he says.

"What happened to our son?" Mom asks, shaking her head. "I want him back, the one that loves to eat, the one that's happy, the one that—"

"When or if you see him, let me know," says Dad. "I want him to prove Arty wrong."

"What are you talking about?" I ask.

"The day you were discharged, when Arty was talking with me, before you approached us to leave," Mom says, "Arty told me 'He'll be back. I've seen this too many times before.' I didn't want to believe him. 'No, not our Gary. You don't know our son. He's strong. He has a great amount of self-discipline. He's able to overcome a great deal of pressure.' Well, I guess Arty was right. Maybe we really don't know our son after all."

Mom gathers dishes and gently clanks them into the kitchen sink. Dad rushes to finish up his third helping of salad and retreats to the garage to regain his sanity. Dessert is canceled—an unheard-of occurrence at the Grahl residence. I remain at the table alone, wholly distraught.

There isn't a time I can recall in recent memory when I felt so disturbed, so highly insignificant. No one seems to think I'm capable of anything on my own. We need to protect our precious, helpless little Gary. I'm so sick of this place!

You're a corrupt, manipulating little monster out of control.

"I can't stand this anymore," says Mom, running the water to do dishes. "I really don't know you. You're sick. You're going back to your stupid little hospital unit tomorrow morning."

I sense tentacles circulating and gagging my conscience. Urges to do unspeakable harm to myself beg for attention. I've hit bottom. My parents hate me. I have no identity, no purposeful reason to keep wasting other people's air.

No one cares.

I wish I had cancer.

Go ahead and wallow in your pity party.

I want to be dead.

Quietly, I get up from the table with my plate of food and set it on the counter. Most nights, I help Mom dry dishes. Tonight, I have never been born. It's so incredibly bad that I even snatch a box of Twinkies from the pantry without Mom noticing and debate about doing something unthinkable. I resolutely make my way to my bedroom and delicately click the door shut. I grab my baseball bat. Smash! One less trophy for Mom to dust, but one more hole in the drywall for Dad to repair.

I sneak into the bathroom and anxiously step up onto the scale. Only 104 pounds? Not bad. I'm getting closer.

What about those Twinkies, Sherlock? Go ahead and make yourself feel worse.

Without a second thought, I tear into the box, rip open a wrapped Twinkie and stuff it into the back of my throat. I don't even chew as I virtually swallow the thing whole. Another goes in, then another. I don't care what happens to me or how I'll feel. For the next three hours of my evening, I punish my body with an unbroken sequence of agonizing exercises with no rest periods. My *Rambo* soundtrack pounds against my eardrums, injecting my muscles with adrenaline. I taste blood. Dehydrated cells squeal for water.

None may be ingested until you're scheduled to lay your head upon your bedtime pillow.

My throbbing feet step onto the flat bathroom scale one final time before my abbreviated visit with Mr. Sandman. My parched throat yearns to chug refreshing, cool water. The zipping dial rests on 103 pounds.

Better, but you're not there yet. No water. It only adds weight.

"Are you all packed for tomorrow?" says Mom, checking in as soon as I snap the lights off.

"I'll do it in the morning," I say in a raspy voice, hopping into bed, critically dehydrated. "Do you have that pair of military pants washed, the one with lots of pockets?"

"Yes, in your drawer."

"Thanks," I mumble, feeling sorry for my family's plight. I pull the covers up to my neck and mercilessly obsess about the Twinkies sitting in my stomach like saturated sponges. "You know, Mom, I don't mean to hurt—"

The door shuts.

Well, good night to you, too. At least she closed the door for once.

CHAPTER TWENTY-SEVEN
BACK SO SOON?

During mandatory check in, my right wrist gets strapped with a bright red security bracelet distinctly characteristic of those residing on Unit 13, displaying to all within eyeshot that I am to be carefully managed, like a highly toxic chemical. I mope along at a snail's pace, dragging my suitcase along behind me. Its metal grommets scrape the floor, sounding like fingernails grating a chalkboard.

"Gary, pick up your suitcase," snaps Mom. "It's gouging the floor, for heaven's sake." She pauses to check the floor for damage. "Darn it! You've left scars!"

Wonderful. Toss it on the pile with the rest of my collection.

Distorted voices over radio transmitters echo within the corridors just down the corridor behind us. They're heading our way. Two armed police officers race past us in fury. "Excuse us, please."

Ariel emerges holding open the unit's door. The officers race in. There's a high-pitched scream followed by a thud, and then the door shuts upon the officers' disappearance to the scene of the crime—everything one perfectly choreographed motion.

"Good morning!" says Ariel, tinkering with one of the seven earrings lining the crest of her ear. "How are you both doing today?" She peaks into the thick glass window for a quick check at the apparent chaos within.

"Great," says Mom, who's all smiles.

"Great," I repeat.

"You'll have to excuse the interruption. We're in the middle of a minor crisis. No big deal. It will only be a minute."

A brief uncomfortable silence tags along. My arm and shoulder plead for a respite from the cumbersome suitcase. I decided to carry it the last twenty yards down the corridor, not out of obedience to Mom's orders, which she thought I was doing, but in an attempt to burn a few last calories before climbing in to an exercise-free unit. I set it down in relief.

"So, how was your trip here?" asks Ariel. "Any problems?"

We shake our heads no. Silence sets in again. Ariel takes another gander into the window. Mom stands patiently, still smiling like a beauty pageant victor.

"Don't you usually work nights?" I ask.

"Yes, but Greta put me on days beginning today. I'm looking forward to finally seeing more action."

The unit door finally opens. I wrap my fingers around the suitcase handle and slowly amble to the front desk of the nurse's station.

"Well, hello there, young man," bellows Wal-Mart. "It's good to see you again. Hi, Mom..."

Mom? I don't see the family resemblance.

"Throw that whopper up here and let's have a little looky, shall we? You didn't pack your knife collection this time did you?"

What?

My skin heats up like a microwave. I give a half-hearted smile and exert three spirited attempts at hoisting my bag onto the counter using two hands, failing miserably each time. I feel lightheaded. That's what I get for loading my stomach with nothing but Twinkies for the last ten hours.

I tried the old puke routine, but was once again unsuccessful. Oh, well. I deserve to feel worse, anyhow.

"Here let me help you with that, Gary," says Mom. "You're so weak you can hardly—"

"Thanks, but I got it, Mom."

A surge of rage inspires my foot to give the bottom of the suitcase a swift kick, thereby helping me to...fail a fourth time. Mom heaves my bulky suitcase up onto the counter with a quick wheeze, using only one arm.

Wal-Mart opens my case and begins her inspection. She rummages through underwear, plain T-shirts, magazines, and sweatpants. I feel like I'm sweating bullets and cover my hand over a bulky pocket. "You check out just fine, dear. Ariel will escort you to your room. Greta and Hadie will catch up with you shortly." She motions toward the Quiet Room. "They're tending to more immediate business at the moment."

I grab my weighty suitcase without looking into Wal-Mart's eyes, feeling wary.

"Oh, and Gary, welcome back," says Wal-Mart.

"Thanks. It's good to be home—"

Mom cringes.

Oops. "I mean back here to get help."

CHAPTER TWENTY-EIGHT

DR. BUCKMIER'S WARNING

All I try to do is be nice to people, to be a good citizen, to stay out of everyone's hair, but something doesn't seem right. God must have missed tightening a nut somewhere when he constructed me.

"Time to weigh in," says Atalanta, leaning on the doorframe to my room. "Let's go. Dr. Buckmier has also ordered a blood test. The phlebotomist will be here shortly."

"Hi, Atalanta." I'm happy to see her.

I enter the exam room, strip, gown, and scrutinize. I've done it so many times I can do it in my sleep. Some people say mirrors do not lie. I think that's poppycock. There's no way I'm as fat as the image it reflects back at me.

Taunt skin grows tight, sending short spouts of tingling all over my body. A concave fissure resides in the center of my chest, and my shoulders look like I swallowed a coat hanger. I have too much neck. A four-inch gap resides between my thighs when my legs are together.

I'm not supposed to weigh myself without staff supervision, but what they don't know won't hurt them. I slide the black iron block across the fulcrum. Dizziness slaps me across the cheek. I go off balance and accidentally fall against an outcrop that supports the scale's measuring instruments, carving a modest gouge into my side.

"Gary—"

I instantly pounce off the scale base.

"—are you ready in there?"

"Yeah."

Chandra told me one time that Atalanta is pushing her mid-to-upper seventies. She's a former drill sergeant turned medic, who, by the looks of her solid frame, still appears to stay in top physical condition. Her world is black and white with no shades of color in between.

"It took you long enough to get changed. What were you doing, knitting your own gown?"

"Sorry," I say, my cheeks turning red.

She winds the blood pressure cuff around my upper arm almost two revolutions, taking my blood pressure and pulse. The pressure is uncomfortably constricting. Tracking my pulse is a little more of a challenge this morning because of how cold I am. My veins, typically elevated on my skin, have burrowed deep to seek warmth. I have zero body fat.

Will I break my record today? I'm wild with anticipation. Atalanta methodically slides the thick black iron block across the lever. Come on... keep going... keep going...

Atalanta shakes her head and sighs. "What are we going to do with you, young man? This is ridiculous."

Sounds like a good sign to me.

"It appears to be... Let's see, 102 and three quarter pounds."

Yessssssssssssssssssss! I better not celebrate too much. Ninety pounds is where true happiness lies. I breathe out a phony sigh of frustration.

"What's the sigh for?" says Atalanta. "It's becoming your trademark. Somehow I think you like this and you know it. Wait here." She reaches for the doorknob, then pauses and looks back. "Dr. Buckmier will be right in to check you over. Oh, and I wouldn't weight myself again without supervision if I were you."

"Huh? How did—?"

"The iron block indicator was not at zero, and I'm positive I returned it there after I weighed a patient in here five minutes ago."

To my surprise, her glare doesn't appear tainted and reproachful, but disappointed and glum. "You know, when you left here six months ago, I had hopes of you beating the odds. You're so young, so capable, such a talented personality. How come you continue to allow this to dictate your life?"

No answer.

Her posture fires a firm warning, as if she wants her words of wisdom to burn a hole into my psyche. "If that's what you plan to do this time, you're wasting your time, and ours. You know what to do, Gary. It's time to take a leap of faith."

No answer.

A knock comes at the door. The sullen mood is interrupted by a young woman with a tray full of tubes of blood. She takes mine so fast I didn't even feel the poke of the needle.

Atalanta departs with the young vampire, Atalanta shaking her head.

A waste of time says Atalanta—sounds familiar.

I quickly dress and head for My Chair, wanting to be left alone as usual. About one hour into a serious sulking session, I hear, "Good morning to you, sir. It's a chilly one out there today. I apologize for my tardiness. My mind told my body to get up and out the front door this morning, but my body strongly disagreed." My scrawny eccentric psychiatrist laughs, an obnoxious snort. It sounds like a warthog in heat.

He gives me the run-through on the typical medical examination— checking my heart, throat, eyes, skin, reflexes, and a quick fiddling with my genitals. Whoa, Doc, stop playing with the ice cube trays before you come in here next time.

After vigorously scrubbing his hands, he snags my chart and temporarily loses himself in a squall of frantic scribbling. I stand and wait for his next words. My eyelids are heavy. I feel weak. My muscles continue to relax, wholly exhausted, and completely spent. I can hear and feel my heart against my ribs. All I want is a bed. Any bed will do. I believe I've earned a short spell of slackened serenity.

Dr. Buckmier tosses the chart onto a nearby chair, folds his arms, and looks at me with rankled eyebrows. I stare back with a puzzled grin, my eyelids half closed from being dizzy and weak.

"You know, son…"

I smell a lecture coming on.

"…I'm going to be totally honest with you. What I'm about to say is not intended to scare you, but to warn you of the seriousness of your condition. Your vitals are ridiculous. You have a pulse of thirty, dangerously low blood pressure, and you're dehydrated and critically malnourished. You have no body fat—zippo. In fact, your body has resorted to using protein for fuel, the building blocks for muscle development. In other words, your body is beginning to eat itself in order to survive."

My mouth opens up for a lion-sized yawn. The corners crack and sting because I'm so dehydrated. "Your blood work shows anemia and dehydration, and your sodium, potassium, and calcium levels are bottoming out at an alarming rate. It's only a matter of time before your heart gives out." He inhales a large gulp of air and lets it out slowly. "Once again, I don't mean to scare you, but I would probably give you a month—tops. Your heart simply cannot endure the stress. Do you understand what I'm saying?"

I stare straight ahead with a blank cast. "You mean I could…?" A burst of adrenaline spurts through my veins.

"I'm talking possible death here," says Dr. Buckmier, making his best case to impress upon me the seriousness of my state of affairs. "Are you listening to me?"

I'm a steady statue of silence, indifferent to the business at hand.

"Gary?"

I am a Green Beret, a Navy SEAL, able to withstand the worst of conditions anywhere. I could die? Awesome.

"You're going to have to understand that I will be giving staff permission to do everything possible in order to ensure your safety," says Dr. Buckmier. "At this point, your health is in immediate danger. It was wise that you came here, but you are far from being in the clear, and that might mean a brief bout of harsh living conditions for you here…"

What others choose to call miserable, I call home.

"…something that you might not be comfortable with…"

Bring it on.

"...and it's going to be for your own good, son. You might find yourself hating us, but when your health is in imminent danger, we are not concerned with maintaining a high opinion."

The *Rambo* theme song materializes in my head.

"...and so you might need an IV tube..."

No one can exceed me in exercise and willpower. Endurance is my middle na—IV tube?

"...will remain there for such a period until you regain acceptable internal functioning..."

I have no idea what Dr. Buckmier is talking about, but am too embarrassed to request that he clarify. I'm such a loser.

"I guess I don't understand," I say, attempting to salvage my mistake with a generic comment.

"You are going to be subject to bed rest, with an IV tube for fluids until further notice. If you choose not to eat, you'll need a NG tube as well."

"Come again?" Panic surfaces at the thought of being without options to exercise and move about at will. "What if I have to go to the bathroom?"

"You will use a bedpan. Nurses will relieve you regularly."

How will I exercise? I'll bloat out in no time. I begin cursing myself in my head, wishing I'd never come back here.

"I am sorry, Gary, but you give us no other choice. Your health is in imminent danger and—"

"You mean I have to have a needle stuck in my arm?"

"Actually, it's inserted through the back of your hand. Your high blood sugars and other tests give us reason to believe that you may have diabetes, and—"

"Diabetes?"

I am frozen. Images come banging into my conscience of *Rambo* enduring the agony of getting his chest muscles sliced with a machete by a Vietnamese soldier.

"So when does this start?" I ask.

"As soon as we're finished here," says Dr. Buckmier. "I'll draw up the order and have the necessary staff come and set you up."

The man is serious. I have to do something. This can't be happening.

"Isn't there any other option available?" I plead.

"Not really."

"What if I promise you that I'll eat anything you put in front of me? I'll sit all day. I won't exercise. You can haul me to the bathroom in a wheelchair and have nurses set me on the toilet, watching my every move. I'll do anything."

Dr. Buckmier seems stricken with compassion. I sense he hates this as much as I do... well, not exactly.

"Son, you've been making promises for the last year and a half. You have a mental illness. Your brain is so malnourished that it's not receiving the adequate amount of glucose for it to function properly. Plus, it's not just a matter of how much you eat; it may be what you eat. Diabetes will have you eating an entirely different diet. "

"No, no, no..." I repeat, shaking my head in disillusionment.

"I'm sorry, Gary."

This calls for desperate measures—begging like a homeless person with a tin cup. It seems pitiful, but I foresee no other options at this point.

"Please, Dr. Buckmier. I'll do anything, anything you want. Pleeeeeeeeease! Just don't stick me in bed all day. What if I sit and take the needle instead?"

"That's not typical procedure."

"Can't you change it, just this once?" Optimism comes into sight over the horizon, but it's just a mirage.

"The temptations for you to exercise and swerve off the normal course of your treatment is too high. Plus, it would be more difficult for us to monitor your progress. I'm sorry, but this is the way it's going to have to be for now. It's only temporary."

It might as well be a thousand years for me.

I begin to shake, on the inside and outside. It feels like I've swallowed a ringing alarm clock.

"You're shivering, son," says Dr. Buckmier, gently touching my shoulder, seeking to be reassuring, "because you have no body fat and your blood sugars are low. But we'll make sure to take care of you."

My blood pressure rises. My heartbeat skyrockets, pressing forth into the red zone. Anxious breathing speedily intensifies, drying the inside of my mouth like desert sand.

Doesn't this feel great? It's the gratifying smell of success at its best.

Shortly after, I'm escorted to my room and hooked up to an IV tube. I've never been more weak and anxious at the same time in my life. Unit 13 staff eye me like hungry hawks in search of prey. Every muscle in my body aches to get up and exercise, but I can't because of this confounded ball and chain of an IV machine. It makes a constant, irritating clicking sound that is surely going to drive me to the brink of insanity.

I call my parents to tell them the bad news, and brace myself for a pair of matching lectures. Surprisingly, I'm spared the sermons but hear an awful lot of heavy sighing and "What else is going to go wrong with you?" repeated over and over.

I found it takes forever to eat lunch and dinner, and I don't even eat everything on my tray; my stomach vehemently protests. I feel like a bulky lump of cumbersome flesh. Greta shows mercy and grants me permission to bypass my bedtime snack. Instead, she sends up a nurse from another unit to educate me about being diabetic.

You are so screwed up.

You have to get your jabs in, too, don't you?

Of course.

CHAPTER TWENTY-NINE

WET DREAM

Ahead of me lies a tapestry of a seemingly endless forest bordered by a dreary haze. The only audible sound is the crunching of my sore feet on scorched brush in a barren wasteland. I inhale a stench so ghastly that I almost puke. I have been overtaken by a disturbing, unexplainable force.

I throw up something awful. Unlike the reward of relief that generally follows the expulsion of vile stomach contents, my vomiting only increases my sickening desire for more. I am weak. An empty soul. This is too much for me to handle.

Dimness gives way to a faint, orange–red glow illuminating the inside of a triangular isolated room. My body involuntarily squeezes into it. Three drab walls topped with the plush satin of a coffin grip my nerves with a claustrophobic fear. Heavy breathing comes about. Haunting eyes hover. IT wants a raw experience.

Welcome back, my friend. Welcome back. It's been so long since your last visit.

I am unable to speak, although my thoughts flow freely.

Why do you torment me? What have I ever done to deserve this?

Self pity—it's one of your more lucrative weapons.

Deep within me bubbles an urge to cry, unable to make its way to the surface.

I haven't heard from you in quite some time.

I beg to differ. I have been with you the entire time. My supremacy has become so much a part of every aspect of your being that you can't tell the difference between me and your own thoughts anymore. I have designed you this way.

My nostrils continue taking in ever-increasing doses of a putrid aroma. I can't think. I don't dare feel. My mind has no memory of family, friends, or human existence—only desolation, despondency, and misery.

I am alone, utterly alone.

This is what you've wanted after all, to be alone.

Then, out of the blue, two words release into my conscience: Help me. They are repeated over and over, strong and somewhat relieving, as if I somehow made them come to my awareness.

Look up.

My chin is forced upward as I take notice of strange markings inscribed on the wall. The three walls slowly begin to close in on me. The claustrophobic fear intensifies, along with the incessant ache in my muscles. My eyelids stretch wide and firm in witness to one word inscribed in a thick, opaque substance that sends sheer terror through my every nerve.

S-H-A-M-E.

You are sinful, disgraceful, and bad. Why do I put up with your bungling mistakes? You can't do anything right. Just stay out of my way.

No! Nooooo! Leave me alone whatever you are!

I writhe about, attempting to free my hands from IT's overpowering clutches.

You have chosen your own destiny.

Me? What are you blaming me for?

This will not be pleasant.

If it wasn't for your miserable directions, I'd be...

Be what? Go ahead and tell me.

I'd be... I'd be...

Come on. I'm waiting. I haven't got all day. Your sentencing awaits.

I guess I'd be...

Can't do it, can you? Do you know why? Because I am who you are. I am your only recourse for sanity.

I don't know. Maybe—

Don't believe me? Well then, if that's the case, let's carry on with sentencing. This is what you will do...

Diabolical-looking eyes, along with a *Rambo* survival knife, emerge through the wall with wording inscribed in blood. All three walls are now glowing orange–red, and begin compressing in upon my shaking body. I jerk my arms, attempting one final ditch effort to free myself and failing miserably. An excruciating sensation comes forth: cold steel being plunged into my wrist held high above my head like a fisherman holding up and displaying his prized catch. Blood spews down my neck and shirt. The pain is unbearable.

And then, out of the blue, something unusual pops into my awareness.

You don't have to listen to this. You are capable.

What is that?

I am YOU. Call me YOU.

For the first time in what seems like an eternity, I finally belt out two words that squeal in my head: "Help me!"

My eyes flip open as I startle awake to the sitting position. A disturbing evil is still fresh.

Where am I?

Stinging and burning originate from my hand. I hear an irritating clicking. A trail of thin plastic tubing extends out of the back of my hand and flows to a machine next to the bed's side girders.

What the—? Nooooo!

A slow pant turns panicky. Sweat drenches an ugly, faded blue hospital gown.

What's going on here? How come I have—? Oh, gross!

My underwear is soaked with a rancid liquid. Pale moonlight streams through the window, glowing over my bed. I'm sitting dead center in the middle of sheets saturated with urine. What time is it? This is crazy! There's no way I'm lying in bed all day. It will kill me, not to mention that in a matter of days I'll feel like a nursing sow that just delivered a litter of piglets. And that full feeling... yuck! What am I going to do about these sheets? I have to do something.

"Are you okay, Gary?" whispers a hunched old nurse with gray hair. "I'm Mary, your nurse this evening. I heard you scream and I—what's that smell?"

Under the distressing circumstances, I find it quite pointless to attempt a full-blown fib, so I simply state the obvious. "I seem to have wet my bed." My cheeks glow scarlet (both ends!) "Here, I better get up and—"

"No!" roars Mary, pushing me back down into bed. "You stay put. I'll take care of it. You stay in bed."

"But how are you going to change the sheets with me in bed?"

"We have strict orders from Greta to make sure you remain in bed at all times—no matter what. Go ahead and slip off your underpants while I grab a soapy washcloth."

She departs to the bathroom connected to my room as I pull off my sopping wet underpants. To my horror, I notice another translucent, gel-like body fluid adhering to the interior of my underwear.

What the heck was I doing? For the love of God, please don't let her see this!

She returns and hands me a wet washcloth smelling of wild flowers. Great. I'll have privates reeking of Ocean Escapades all day. I wipe my groin and midsection area and drop my briefs into a blood-colored, biohazard-waste bag, which Mary holds at arm's length, treating the contents like a venomous snake. I dare not look at her. It's too mortifying. She hands me a dry pair of underwear she fished out of my drawer and begins helping me undo my hospital gown.

I, Gary Grahl, am totally naked in front of a strange old woman.

She helps me get into a new gown and changed the bed sheets while I stand helplessly next to the IV machine.

I whisper, "What time is it?"

"Two in the morning. I'll take care of the sheets. You get back into bed and sleep."

"Thanks, Mary."

Sleep? Yeah, right. I might as well burn some calories.

I tighten my stomach, curl my arms behind my back, and begin doing sit-ups—five hundred to be exact. I reward myself with short rest periods after every seventy-five repetitions.

I flip to my stomach and begin to pound out the first set of push-ups that will eventually reach three hundred in number. The squishy, uneven surface of the mattress causes my wrists to hyperextend and strain. Despite stinging, I keep going. My arms quake from fatigue. I keep going. The pressure exerting on my wrist joint causes my IV needle to tear slightly from its inserted hole. A trickle of blood drops to my freshly sheeted bed. I keep going, glancing at the door every few seconds to see if the coast is clear. Pain is everywhere. I keep going—going, going, going. It's just the way things are. I've descended to depths that I never thought imaginable. I have plummeted to the likes of filthy vermin, inhuman, unworthy to show genuine kindness and mercy to myself. There's no way I'm touching food at this point.

I flip over onto my back and rest, panting hard.

I don't want to tramp down the long road to health. It's too complex, too unfamiliar, too many uncomfortable feelings involved. There's nothing conceivably left to live for. I want cancer. I want to suffer a slow, painful death. Then again, I'm getting one right now. But it's not painful enough—

TIME OUT!

"Gary?" whispers Mary. "Are you awake?" She's twenty-five minutes early for her rounds.

I lie still as if in a deep slumber, forcing my breaths so my body looks like it's relaxed. She tip toes over to my bedside and leans in close to my face, making sure I'm for real. She's had Doritos for a snack. My counterfeit snoring wins me my second Academy Award.

The door slowly eases closed to a crack, back to darkness.

YOU? You saved me.

Yeah, Mary almost caught you. That was close.

I'm not referring to Mary.

CHAPTER THIRTY

CAN'T YOU SEE THE "NO TRESPASSING" SIGN?

"**Y**ou had us scared for a moment," says Greta. She sits at the end of my bed.

I look puzzled. "What do you mean?"

"Your vitals, with Dr. Buckmier. They were dangerously low. And when you got all worked up, well, that just made things worse."

I shake my head in disillusionment, hardly believing this is all happening to me..

"Blood tests showed severe dehydration and anemia, causing lightheadedness. You could have passed out on the street somewhere and been in serious trouble. It could have been fatal. Someone is certainly looking out for you.

"Do you think it could have caused the nightmare I had last night?" I ask.

Greta nods her head. "Possibly. Fluctuating body chemistry can cause all sorts of weird things to happen to you, the least of which can be a nightmare."

We sit in silence for a few moments. I consider sharing the details of my dream with her, but refrain from doing so at the last minute. It was too creepy.

"Are you okay, Gary?" asks Greta.

How does she always know? "Yeah, everything is fine," I lie.

Oh, great. There's that look in her eye again. She's up to something. I just know it.

"No, I mean, is everything okay with you?"

"Yeah—really. Why?"

Can't you read the sign? It says no trespassing.

Her silent gaze tells me she's not convinced. Greta is known for her keen intuitive wits. She can read right through any con artist, particularly the wiles of someone protecting an eating disorder. After Arty, she's been my toughest challenge. I think she really does know exactly how the gears turn inside my head. I hope so, because I don't.

"You're a tough cookie, aren't you?" she says.

Green Beret all the way. Don't you forget it.

It's time to stop listening to your eating disorder messages. They're lies.

Don't pay any attention to that...that...thing.

"Well," she says meditatively, now folding her arms, "I'm glad that you're happy."

Huh?

"Your clever resourcefulness, your sheer willpower and drive, your dogged self-discipline—admirable qualities, are they not? I'm glad you seem at home with them."

My smile turns aloof. "Thanks...I think."

"Of course, considering the present circumstances, I'm not entirely convinced they're helping you get where you really want to go."

Really? Well, I—

"What do you think?" she asks inquisitively, lowering her chin to gaze at me over her gaudy black spectacles resting low on her nose.

I shrug my shoulders. "I don't know."

"I see." Greta was obviously hoping for a more in-depth reply.

At first, I contemplate whether or not I've made the right move by not spilling my guts to her. It felt so good in group therapy with Arty.

You worked hard for that. You took a risk and it paid off for you. Keep going.

But feeling good is not in my future at the moment.

"Well, suit yourself." She slaps her hands to her thighs, gets up, makes her way to the door, pauses, and then turns with a pondering grin. "You know, Gary, we are not the enemy. My hope is for you to soon come to understand that it's in your best interest not to add to the arsenal of your eating disorder."

I smile back. Her words bounce off me like super balls hitting concrete.

She winks. "Oh, by the way, we've decided that once you're off this IV, it would be in your best interest to begin eating in the cafeteria—alone. You'll have a meal pass to get you in. We'll talk more later."

But, but...my menu. I like my menu.

"Have a good day."

CHAPTER THIRTY-ONE

THE POWER OF YOU

Thanksgiving is here. It's the first time I fail to do turkey with my family. It feels awfully strange, like I accidentally hopped the wrong plane and ended up in a foreign country. As I think about it, I have to admit I enjoy the camaraderie with family, though I don't miss the stomach- inflating meal. Instead, I find myself sitting (lying actually) alone in a room on a psychiatric unit, hooked up like jumper cables to a noisy engine.

Oh, God, how much longer must I endure this dreadful existence? This stupid eating disorder is not making me any happier in the least.

Hey! Watch your language, boy! I got you out of prom, didn't I?

Then an astonishing turn of events happens. Dr. Buckmier notices that over the last two days my blood sugars have stabilized, without every meal being lower in sugar. He studies my chart carefully and comes to the conclusion that I don't have diabetes after all. Upon further inspection, he realizes he didn't take into consideration my Twinkie binge only hours before my admission. I guess it would have helped if I told him this tiny bit of information in the first place. Whoops.

"Atta boy, Gary," says Ariel. "'Fessing up really has its advantages, doesn't it? Now the IV can come out. Let's celebrate with a game of Scrabble."

"I'll even let you have a twenty-point lead," says Ariel.

"Bite me."

"Now that's what I like to hear—a little spunk."

Ariel is cool. She may seem a little weird at times, but she's an experienced nurse and knows how to handle teenagers. She's been killing time with me playing Scrabble for the last two days. She's up six games to one, and she's never at a loss for witty comebacks. Her philosophies of life are "Grab life by the flanks and chew" and "I can do it. Just get the heck out of my way." I think she's beginning to rub off on me. My anorexia idiosyncrasies don't seem to faze her, and she treats me like I'm her college roommate. I like the free-falling companionship. It's uncensored and spontaneous, and she's not the least bit interested in psychoanalyzing me. This is new for me.

Dad pays me a visit after the Thanksgiving gorging at the Grahl house. Ariel says she'll check in on me later. Mom is conveniently absent, as if she sent Dad with a written excuse saying: *Dear Teacher, I am unable to come to the unit because I have too many dishes to wash. Please send messages with Dad. Love, Mom.* I think her absence has something to do with the IV sticking out of her son.

"We all miss you at home," says Dad. "Dinner's not the same without you."

"I'll bet."

Dad is a new person when he visits me on the unit. For one, he actually sits down and listens to me and wants to talk. At home, he talks to his favorite companions: buzz saws, a hammer and nails, and roofing shingles. Generally, the only words I hear from him are "Could you hand me that reciprocating saw?" or "Watch where you're walking—there's windows down there."

He pulls up a chair next to my bed. "How's the food up here?"

"Good."

"I see you're off that tube thing already. That's great."

"Yeah," I say. "Dr. Buckmier didn't realize that I—" I pause, debating whether or not I should tell Dad about my Twinkie adventure. I feel like a magician unwilling to reveal the secret to my magic tricks.

"Realize what?"

"Uh, nothing. Say, I hear the Brewers are going to have better pitching this season."

"Really?" says Dad. He gives me a curious look, but doesn't challenge me.

"Yeah," I say. "Maybe they'll fight their way out of the cellar this year, considering the money these guys make. That's just ridiculous. How can a human being..."

We bump around sports gossip for awhile, avoiding the proverbial elephant in the room. It's our way of comforting ourselves. But then for some unknown reason, maybe because he ingested too much cranberry sauce, Dad changes his tune and decides to talk.

"You know, Gary, I was thinking... Sometimes I get the notion that you play baseball because you think it's something I want you to do."

I go rigid.

"I just want you to do something *you* want to do. You don't have to play baseball if you don't want to."

The only part of my body that wants to move is my lips to smile. "No, of course not," I answer with vigor. "I love playing baseball. It's something I enjoy very much."

Be honest with him. He knows already anyhow.

"It just seems like you're not playing because you like playing," says Dad, giving me another chance to 'fess up. "Maybe I'm wrong, I don't know."

IT won't let me—or is it, I won't let myself?

IT does not need to determine what you say, how you feel, or how you act. Just let go and speak what you feel right now.

Please don't make me do this, YOU. I can't.

Yes, you can. You're capable.

No, I'm not.

Yes, you are. You're just not used to it right now.

"I'm not playing just for you," I say with forged confidence. "I play because it's fun."

Dad just stares at me like he doesn't know what else to do.

Your window of opportunity has been opened. Go with it.

I stare back... and think... and look down... and think... then out the window... and think...

"Hey, Dad?"

"Yeah?" He's all ears. No screeching buzz saws, wailing hammers, or arguing with two-by-fours.

"Well..."

Go ahead.

Sorry, YOU. I just can't. I'm such an—

No, you're not an idiot. You're a boy holding onto anorexia. It's okay that you want to struggle with this longer. If it's your prerogative right now, there's nothing anyone can do about it. But there are other more enjoyable ways of coping.

Like what?

Well, like talking to your dad, for instance. Your eating disorder likes to lie and tell you it's too painful to share your feelings. Look at it this way: If your eating disorder were telling the truth, that would mean everyone else would be lying to you. Do you honestly believe half the nation is out to pull one over on you?

Well, no. Now that you mention it, if I could be happy without IT—

Your eating disorder, that is.

Oh, yeah, sorry, my eating disorder, I'd dive for the opportunity—

Your prison door stands open right now.

—and staff keeps reminding me how my eating disorder is not me—

Correct. Your anorexia is not who you are.

—but, it's just so hard—

IT is a liar, remember?

So, you're saying giving up my anorexia is not hard?

No, your anorexia says recovery is not possible. Change will be difficult, but it's energizing and meant for your good, not your downfall. You need to stop putting all your money on the deceptive messages of your eating disorder and begin trusting in other people's time-honored, respected opinions—starting with your own.

I have no opinions.

No, you've simply been told you're not allowed to have your own opinions.

You mean I can give myself permission to have opinions?

Yes, of course. It's one of the wondrous benefits of personal choice.

But how?

Don't try so hard. Let go. Just do. React according to your intuition. Don't let your anorexic ways beat you to the punch. Experiment. Hang loose.

Let me try something...

"Dad?" I say impatiently. "I gotta tell you something." A foreign thought picks away at my conscience. "I have to be honest with you..."

That's it. Say it before the old tapes in your head have a chance to screw it up.

Dad perks up like a dog listening for a rustle in the bushes.

"You're right," I continue, "I haven't been having fun with baseball." The confession keeps flowing. "It's been a chore for a long time. I don't want to disappoint you or anything, but—"

"Oh, no, of course you're not disappointing me, Gary," says Dad with a hearty chuckle. "I just want you to be happy, that's all. You can do or be anything you want to be."

Swwoooooooooooooooosh! Score.

A warm, exhilarating waterfall cascades over my conscience. The unmistakable relief I felt in group therapy with Arty returns. I'm actually feeling it again!

"I guess I was afraid that you would be disappointed in me if I wanted to take a break from sports."

"No, of course not. As long as it's something you want to do." There's a brief pause, and then, "So, you don't like playing sports?"

Aha! See, you've disappointed him.

You don't know that for sure. Whatever he's feeling, he can cope with it on his own. He's been dealing with his own feelings for longer than you've been alive. He can handle it.

"No, I love playing sports," I clarify. "It's just that I've grown up with the reputation of being good in sports and everyone expects me to keep participating in them and being successful."

"I don't believe everyone thinks that, Gary," Dad says. "I don't know how you've come to believe that, because I think that's a lie."

Told you.

"Not everyone walks around with your picture on a video camera hoping to view what Gary Grahl's going to do next," continues Dad. "They have their own lives to worry about, and don't expect you to be any more perfect than they are. In fact, what usually happens is that while you're busy thinking about how much they're judging you, they're looking at you and thinking how much you're judging them. Do you?"

"Well, no."

Dad sits back and folds his arms. "Well now, there you go."

Good point.

I've never examined the details of this principle under this much light before. My eating disorder tapes in my head are typically all over me by now. Speaking of tapes, how come I'm not hearing them all of a sudden?

The power of choice is wonderful, isn't it?

I feel like I want to send home my own letter to Mom: *Dear Mom: I gave Dad messages for you. We talked today! Please see him for details. Wish you were here. Love, Gary.*

CHAPTER THIRTY-TWO

AN IDOL VISIT

"I just can't seem to get these buttons fastened," says Stanley, an older gentleman who was admitted yesterday with clinical depression. He attempts to button his flannel shirt. "The cuffs on the sleeves are a bit short. It's so hard to get the little button in the hole."His hands quiver uncontrollably. I wonder if he's a lifetime coffee drinker, too. "Ha, ha, ha...If only I had my wife here right now, ha, ha, ha... How come the darn thing won't—*blast it all*! Why doesn't this—Arghhhh! This stupid, confounded button, ha, ha, ha... Why can't this country make something as simple as a—*dang it*!"

"Stanley!" interjects Arty. "Let's try and keep a cool head. It's okay to ask for assistance if you need it."

The low rumbling chuckle ripples around the room like The Wave at a Brewers game. It's my first group therapy session since being readmitted more than a week and a half ago. Doreen sits across from Arty as usual, eyeing prospective candidates for a therapeutic lashing. Who will fall victim today? How about a guy who calls himself "Booty," even though Arty calls him by his real name, Joe? Leave Floyd the Felon alone. What about greasy-haired, Angel of Death Girl all decked out in black with the wrist wrapped in heavy gauze? I overheard patients whispering that she was the subject of all the raucous a few days ago when I was admitted. At least I think it's a girl. It's hard to tell with all that black hair shading her face.

"You're back," says Arty, giving me his characteristic stare.

"Yup."

Arty lifts his eyebrows as if persuading me to elaborate. I stay in my own back yard.

"Care to say anything about it?" he says.

"Well, I'm still struggling with my anorexia, but somehow I believe I'm really getting better."

He glances at Angel of Death Girl, who refuses to take her eyes off the carpeting. She begins chewing her lip. A brief silence ensues with sniffing, a cough here and there, and a yawn or two.

Arty tries again. "I'm wondering if the same strategy that worked for you last time might work for you this time, too. What do you think, Gary?"

Hey, I wasn't looking for a stage.

Practice what you've learned, remember?

You're right, although I'm only going so far today.

It's your call.

"Well, it's like this. I was discharged around six months ago and was feeling pretty confident..."

For the next ten minutes, I share my guilt, my lying, my humiliation over letting others down, everything—well, everything except the details of my disturbing dream a few days ago. I'm not ready to reveal that secret. But I must admit that my eating disorder takes a back seat when YOU talks. Doreen is stunned by my self-disclosure. Arty keeps shooting Angel of Death Girl glances between my admissions of heart. He's working her. I run out of gas.

"You're doing great, Gary," encourages Doreen.

You know, to be honest, I actually am feeling relieved, and a bit more confident with—

Knock, knock, knock.

Heads turn toward the group door window. Ariel's face is cut in half (she's on the short side) waving for someone to come out, but I can't tell—me? You want me? But strict Unit 13 rules do not allow patients out of group unless it's a life or death emergency. The door pries open.

"Excuse the interruption, everyone. Gary?" Ariel pulls her finger like a trigger. "You have a special visitor, Gary."

"I thought we weren't allowed visitors during the day," I say, walking down the corridor with Ariel, "especially during group time."

Ariel beams a sly smile, and says, "You're right. But, I think in this case, we can make the exception."

I wonder... Is Chandra here again? A lively cluster of staff and patients blocks the entrance way to the waiting room. Some are holding out pens and pieces of paper as if wanting autographs. As Ariel and I approach, staff and patients part in two, like the Red Sea did for Moses. Jealousy spreads all over their faces.

I round the corner and—

Jim Gantner stands in front of me. "Hi, Gary. How ya doin'?" He finishes an autograph for Hadie. Another tall, tanned, middle-aged man steps forward and extends his hand. "Gary, I'd like for you to meet Pastor Ike Mason," Jim says, "from the church my family and I attend down in Milwaukee."

We shake and share greetings. Scattered whispering continues to flutter around me. Atalanta works her Marine Corps skills. "For crying out loud, folks, let's not suffocate our honored guests. They need oxygen, not your carbon dioxide. Get back to business. Move it! Move it! Let's go, let's..."

Jim leans over and whispers to me, "Is there somewhere private we can visit for a little while?"

"Yeah, sure," I say, leading them away from the mob. "We can use my room."

This is absolutely unheard of. I can hardly believe I'm getting a private visit from one of my all-time favorite baseball heroes. I pinch myself to make sure it's not a dream. Ouch. Nope.

"Nice room they set you up with here," says Jim, glancing around the room.

I stand frozen to my spot, still in a state of disbelief. Jim seems much shorter than when I watch him on television. He's lean with broad shoulders and has forearms like a blacksmith. His speech is direct and with a very firm conviction, similar to his gutsy style of running the bases.

"So how did you find out about me?" I ask.

"Your dad told me you were up here. A great guy, your father is. So is your mother. They're worried sick about you, and love you very much. We go way back, me and your dad. When I was a little kid, he used to invite me over to mess around with him and his baseball team in town. I couldn't get enough of it. He was always so patient and nice to me when others weren't. I never forgot that. We sort of developed a bit of a friendship, but lost touch when I got older."

He glances out the window before turning back to me. "I heard about your tryout. Good for you. Mr. Blitzke told me about you being pretty good, so he decided to give you a look." Jim pulls up a chair and sits down on it backwards, leaning forward against the back. "So what's this I hear about you having anorexia?"

Pastor Ike was looking out over the grounds, but now he's working his way back toward Jim and me. "Yes, what's going on?"

At first, I have trouble thinking clearly, but I slowly find my voice again. "I struggle with being afraid to gain weight. I look in the mirror and want to be skinnier, but I just can't seem to stop it. It's like there's this voice in my head telling me that I'm worthless and incapable of being good at anything. I'm so sick of it."

Jim intently listens. "Wow, it sounds miserable if you feel required to take orders from an invisible force. So you believe you're fat?"

"Well, it's more like I'm not skinny enough. My muscles feel bloated and flabby a lot. I hate that feeling. I just wish I could be normal like everyone else."

"Me, too," says Jim, nodding his head. Pastor Ike pulls up a chair next to Jim.

"How so?" I ask. "It must be nice to be you."

"Well, I can't deny that playing a game I love in the best ballparks in the world has many advantages, and the money's not bad, either," Jim says, "but there's a price to pay, too."

"Price?"

"Yeah, I'm away from my family ten months out of the year, I never know if I'll have a job come the following week, and there's lots of temptation on the road to have sex, do drugs and alcohol, and the hotel rooms get pretty old. The glamour was exciting at first, but it wore off a long time ago. There's also the pressure to perform like a superstar every night. Crowds, even at home sometimes, can get pretty nasty if you don't give 'em a good show. If I ever get into a batting slump, it's pure torture. At this level of play, people expect you to come out of it quickly or they start thinking something is wrong with you. The media will jump all over you and play it up worse than it is. I can start to believe this pesky little voice in my head..."

Pesky little voice? Is it the same one I have?

Why don't you ask him?

No, he'd think you're some sort of weirdo or something.

"And if I'm on the road a long way from home in a lonely hotel room with nothing except my slump grilling me in the brain, well... let's just say it's not easy to have a positive major league attitude," he says.

Go ahead and just ask him. Don't think about it—just do it.

No, you better keep your mouth shut or—

"So," I say, determined to ignoring IT, "how do you handle this, uh, voice you talk about?"

"I mock it," says Jim, without hesitation.

"You mock it?"

"Yeah. I learned a long time ago from a, well, let's just call him a buddy of mine that told me it's important to not listen to these haunting messages. My batting slump is not me. They are two separate things. So when I'm up to the plate after going a few nights without a hit and words like 'Loser!' or 'You're going to strike out again...' get the best of me, I start talking to myself. The catcher and umpire think I'm nuts, and sometime they even tell me so, but I don't care."

Jim's voice is confident and strong, as if he's trying to make every pore in my skin absorb the exact attitude and meaning he's trying to convey. I can't help but think he's probably made this speech dozens of times to other patients he's visited over the years. Why would he choose me?

That's a good point. Why would he choose to waste his valuable time on a no-name lowlife like you?

That's not yours to determine or control. The fact is that he's here right now, taking the time with you and no one else.

I sit focused and still, trying with all my might to disregard the irritations of IT and remember ever single word uttered from Jim's mouth. I don't want to miss any of it.

"I joke along with them," continues Jim. "I make a game out of it. I say things to the voice like 'Not this time, Stinky,' or 'See you on second base,' or my all time favorite is to simply laugh out loud. I concentrate really hard on staying focused in the moment, reflecting on how much talent and hard work got me where I am in the first place, and let go of the situation, giving it to God. It's called Vigor for Living. The voice backs off, and most of the time, I rip a hit up the middle."

Pastor Ike remains quiet but attentive with his arms folded, leaning back in his chair. He nods his head a lot at Jim's words.

"You make it sound so easy," I say, still trying to grasp the marvel of having Jim Gantner here in front of me, in my room, talking to me.

"It's not, though. It takes lots of patience and practice. But the main thing is that I don't allow myself to wallow in pity, or at least for very long. It's one of the enemy's favorite weapons."

Take responsibility for yourself right now.

"What did you say is Vigor for Living?"

Pastor Ike clears his throat, "I think I can answer that one."

He hands me a thin booklet with "Vigor for Living" written boldly on the top. "It's all in there."

"It's all about taking our eyes off our own selfish, shallow, imperfect perspectives of life and looking through God's spy glass," says Pastor Ike. His voice is soft, but his face lights up. He's really passionate about this. "We will never be 'good enough,' as people say. Vigor for Living is the reward for giving control up to God—no matter how badly we've screwed up or how awful we think we are. The Bible says that God makes up His own mind about us anyway and loves us, despite all our shortcomings. It's a gift to us, and can't be earned."

Words escape me. I've always perceived God as a policeman, not a friend. Come to think of it, I think of everyone as a policeman, ready to pounce on me with unwarranted criticism.

It's time to let go of your pride. It's okay.

Let go, let go, let go... there are those words again. What the heck is letting go?

Pastor Ike continues, "I view it as a major swallowing of my pride on a daily basis. I like to think that I know how to run my life, and sometimes I'm arrogant enough to believe I'm an authority on how others should conduct their lives. But reality says otherwise. It's accepting the clear fact that I am not the center of the universe. God is bigger than my problems. I need to accept and submit to this fact. Go with it. One of my favorite verses is Romans 12:2, which goes something like, 'Don't be controlled by the patterns of this world, but be metamorphosized by the renewing of your mind', sort of like a butterfly after it comes out of its cocoon."

"Hey, I saw someone holding a sign with that verse on it in a *Sports Illustrated* article about you, Jim.," I say, my tone suddenly energized.

Pastor Ike and Jim both chuckle.

"You mean you see them, too?" says Jim, sticking his arms over his head like he's waving a big sign. "We get a kick out of those guys."

My mind is abuzz, trying to analyze his every word. It's mentally exhausting, but it's worth the fight. I sense bits and pieces of his wisdom breaking through cracks in my pride.

Pastor Ike glances at his watch and shows the face to Jim.

"Gary," says Jim, getting up and putting the chair back, "we hate to cut this short, but we have to get moving along to other business. Can I have your booklet for a moment?"

He clicks a pen he pulled from his pocket and begins writing on the cover. "I'm giving you my home phone and address. If you ever have anymore questions or just want to talk, don't hesitate to give me a call." He finishes the script and hands it back to me. "Before we go, would you be open to praying with us?"

"Sure."

The prayer is brief but heartfelt—something new to me. My brain makes a new file called "Real Prayers."

The front desk is packed with staff I've never seen before. People clipped with ID badges from other departments and outfitted with dark blue pajamas with little booties politely beg for autographs. Even though rushed for time, Jim is happy to sign things like syringes, surgical gowns, and tongue depressors.

"Your bratwurst are waiting for you down in the dining room," comments Atalanta, with one index finger pointing at me and the other aiming down the hall. "They're calling your name. I'd suggest you answer."

Jim and Pastor Ike look at me with amused expressions, then over to Atalanta, then back at me.

"Yeah, okay," I say, waving her off genially. I'm not keen on Atalanta playing the condescending game right now. After some congenial waving and final good-byes, Jim and Pastor Ike scurry out the door. This last fifteen minutes happened quickly, like a surprise birthday party. A contented aura encircles me like a coat of armor. I need to organize, reflect, and bring it all together somehow.

It's time to change, to move on with life.

I think you're right. I'm sick of being sick.

CHAPTER THIRTY-THREE

THE WARNING

Mr. Rueter, my chemistry teacher, officially reports for tutoring detail. He brings me a sack full of homework before breakfast this morning. The only time he could do it was before school, so Greta agreed to bend the "no visitors before the dinner hour" rule again. Ever since my first hospitalization, I have steadily gotten behind in many of my subjects. Ms. Wheeler informed me on the phone that if Unit 13 keeps me away for a time similar to my first tour of duty, I might be in danger of not graduating with my class.

Mr. Rueter and I sit at the dining room table, swimming in a pool of chemistry charts, diagrams, tables, and a NASA calculator. Angel of Death Girl sits quietly by herself at another table playing solitaire. Boy, she's up early. She seems to be following me, showing up in the background wherever I go.

A scream erupts from the other end of the unit. Mr. Rueter's chin pops up like a mole sensing a red-tailed hawk. "What was that?"

Loosen up. Try humor on for size.

"Probably someone being electrocuted," I say, trying with all my might to keep a straight face. "It's a new form of therapy, haven't you heard?"

Mr. Rueter's head fires around at me. "No way, really?"

"Well, anything to cure a patient. You're into science, right? You'd probably find it interesting. You see, they take these special kind of jumper cables and... "

Mr. Rueter's face is ridden with horror. "You're not serious, are you?"

"Psych!" I say.

Angel of Death Girl grunts. I turn red.

Mr. Rueter slaps me hard on the shoulder. "Gary! Don't do that to me!" Seconds later, he uncorks a hearty laugh; however, his explanations on electromagnetic particles get longer. So much for having fun.

You took a risk and went outside of your comfort zone. Good for you.

Mr. Rueter departs with my latest homework under his arm.

Dr. Buckmier finds me before I even put my books away, but surprisingly, it's a brief session. I notice he has almost double the usual number of charts at his feet this morning.

"Enjoy your breakfast," says Dr. Buckmier, almost pushing me out of the sunroom. Today I actually wanted to talk, too. I'm a bit nervous. I eat in the cafeteria for the first time this morning.

I do a quick stop at my room to snag the journal I was ordered to write in after meals. Ariel thought it would be a safe, constructive way to express my feelings. I learn I actually enjoy writing. Maybe I could write a book someday.

I double check to make sure I have the meal pass ID Greta gave me and exit Unit 13 to the basement, where the cafeteria is housed. I walk down a long hallway with windows showing storm gutters and large dumpsters. I've never been down to this part of the hospital. It's housekeeping central: closets galore with bright yellow floor cleaning buckets, mops, "Caution" cones, and a chemical factory of disinfectants. Delicious smells are ahead.

The cafeteria has a half dozen cooks slaving away in puffy white hairnets behind two long food counters. Today's menu sits overhead: scrambled eggs, bacon, sausages, and waffles with strawberry glaze. A salad bar is its own separate island in the middle of the room, but instead of salad, it holds dozens of yogurts packed on a large mound of ice. A variety of miniature cereal packages are neatly stacked on a shelf just above the yogurts. A massive beverage subdivision lines the outside walls.

I stand in the center of the room in awe. Food screams at me from all directions, causing me to plug my ears with my index fingers. I act like I'm scratching ear hair so the cafeteria staff doesn't think I'm weird. I'm a foreign visitor to their land.

Just turn around and exit. Go walk around the hospital for half an hour and tell the staff you're full.

They will be checking your meal pass ID.

You're right, plus I'm famished. I'm not passing up a chance to taste some of this scrumptious food I'll never get at home in a million years. I'll choose sparingly. I grab a tray and begin my commission.

"Hello," I say to two stout, grandmotherly women with large saggy arms. "My name's Gary. I'm from Unit 13. I'll be taking meals down here for a while. I have a meal pass ID." I hold it up for their inspection as they closely examine its authenticity. Without taking eyes off me, they lean in toward each other and mumble like Chip and Dale, the Disney chipmunks. They return to standing position, which is close to the same height as when they leaned over, and say, "Oh, that's nice."

What to choose, what to choose...

"I think I'll have a very small portion of scrambled eggs, please," I say. "And make it a very small portion."

With nervous anticipation, I closely scrutinize one of the women scoop up a bucket-sized spoon full of eggs. She begins to dump."

"No! Wait!" I roar. That's too much."

The woman jumps, spilling half the contents onto the overhanging heat shield. "Oh, for Pete's sake!"

"Sorry about that," I say, feeling extremely self-conscious. "I'll take what's left in the spoon, that'll be fine."

She dumps the rest onto my plate.

"Wait!"

She bumps the spoon onto the plastic overhang again.

"I'll take a small waffle instead, please. Sorry about that."

"Well, I can't really scrape the eggs off now," says the woman, obviously perturbed. "I'd have to throw it out."

You will not eat that. It has too many calories.

That little extra will not make you fat.

I attempt to send subliminal messages, staring compellingly at both women. "Well... I..."

Cafeteria codes take precedence. "Here," says the woman, who, to my utter horror, hands me the plate. "If you don't want to eat the rest, just leave it on your plate."

A rush of anxiety shivers through me. It does not exactly fit to my caloric specifications. I need an unblemished plate. You were stationed here per Greta's orders, weren't you? This is some sort of ploy to manipulate me into eating more than I want, isn't it?

"Thanks, ladies," I say with a vibrant smile. "Have a good day."

I grab a bowl of Raisin Bran, chocolate milk, and a small carton of orange juice and head to the checkout. The cashier questions my meal pass ID at first. She excuses herself to check it out with management. I stand and scan the forest of tables situated in a triangular pattern within the vast eating area.

Everyone is staring at you.

No they aren't. They're focused on enjoying their own conversations.

Hospital employees are scattered, some looking back at me as if trying to catch details of the disturbance taking place at the cashier's station. The cashier returns with a tall, spiffily-groomed gentleman with shiny hair. He carefully analyzes my ID.

"Yeah," says the man, flipping my ID back and forth, "this is the guy Unit 13 called about. Run him through."

Look! Now you're angering the busy employees piling up in line behind you. You're simply an annoyance to everyone.

They'll survive. Life is not perfect. They can handle their own issues.

I go into hiding at a small table in the far corner of the cafeteria. Now for something to read. It helps to draw out my meal time. For some odd reason, memorizing box scores comforts me. I love to analyze statistics like free throw percentages, earned run averages, and which NHL team claims the best road record. I notice a rack full of newspapers and magazines over by the coffee machines, so I hurry over to hopefully snatch today's sports page. I rummage through a scruffy pile of Saint Abernathy Bugler papers but, alas, the latest edition is last week's. I'll make do.

Nibble, nibble, taste, taste, lick, lick. It takes me five minutes just to swallow my first full bite of eggs. There's too much on my plate. At least I can scrape and push it onto my tray without being reprimanded by a nurse.

I decide to change the pace and write in my journal. Ariel told me to block out any distractions or inhibitions of the moment and simply write whatever comes to my mind or heart. I hesitate, wanting to write the perfect journal entry. I don't want to mess up the nice new pages. Here goes:

Dear God,

This is my very first journal entry. I'm unsure of what to write, but I thought you would be a good person to address it to. I feel like a bloated pig, even though others say I'm as skinny as a flag pole. When I look in the mirror, I know I'm not extremely obese or anything, but I can't see how others think I'm so thin. I don't think I'm thin enough. I feel fat all the time, except when I'm hungry, and even during some of those times I still feel this horrible "fat" feeling within my muscles. I wish I didn't have to be like this. Others can't seem to understand that it's not my fault. They think I can just stop it cold turkey. But it's not that easy. I really want to get better and wish I could, but for some reason I'm stuck in a hole and can't seem to crawl back out. The sides are too slippery.

The eggs and milk seem to be laughing at me. They stare up at me and make jokes of my wimpy nature. I HATE IT! Why can't I think normally, eat normally, feel normally, and live a normal life? My family has been so supportive and I feel like I'm letting everyone down.

I want desperately for a girl to like me—to have a real girlfriend—but I don't know if I'll ever get there. Who would want to go out with me anyhow? I'm such a freak with this stupid eating disorder. I'm tired of exercising in secret and I'm tired of always feeling like I MUST exercise to burn calories. But I'm afraid if I stop, I'll start to gain all this weight and feel terribly full and fat. Everything will get out of control.

I like this new YOU voice deep inside me. It helps me keep my eating disorder at bay.

Please help me, God. Jim Gantner and Pastor Ike told me that I need to rest my trust with you. How do I exactly do that? How do I "let go" or "give the situation to you?"

I better get going for now. Please send help.

Love, Gary

I chug down the orange juice, eat my last spoonful of Raisin Bran, and throw away my trash, feeling somewhat satisfied. Anything other than biting hunger after a meal used to be forbidden by my personal eating laws, but many weeks of Atalanta's surveillance of my every move at the Unit 13 dining room table is beginning to wear into my habits. I find I can handle more food and it's not as big a deal.

You think you can run up and down the stairs five full times without stopping?

My tiptoes stand pressed against the bottom of step number one. I glance up the stairwell, contemplating the pain of ten times up and down the steps—all 600 of them. I know the number well.

Go on. You're wasting time.

Use the elevator. You've changed. You don't even care to do this anymore.

I look down at the floor and sigh.

Come on. Move!

Thinking... thinking... thinking...

Let's go. Move your—

No.

Good for you.

What did you say to me?

I said no. I'm tired of this. It hasn't really gotten me any thinner. In fact, the scale told me I gained weight on occasion after exercising wildly in my room. Why am I even doing it anymore? I hate all this exercising. It's a battle that's never satisfied.

You need it. It's mandatory for you happiness.

Happiness comes in many packages, not just exercising and food.

Without another thought, I stride toward the pair of elevator doors near the hospital entrance and hit the "up" button.

You weakling. You're going to get fat.

No, you're not. Pay attention to past experiences. Focus.

Ding. The elevator doors open and I step inside.

You did it! Great job, Gary. You did the right thing. Enjoy the victorious feeling you're having right now.

CHAPTER THIRTY-FOUR

THE INFATUATION BEGINS

Since staff is allowing more freedom in my protocol because of small, steady weight gains and because I'm talking more in group therapy, I'm not required to be observed after meals. But familiar habits somehow force me down to My Chair after every feeding, where I'm coming to like journaling. I feel better after writing down my innermost thoughts and feelings on paper. My eating disorder loses steam.

Loser.

I'm almost afraid to admit it, but something is happening inside me, and I have no idea where it's coming from.

It's called working hard at talking, making little changes in thinking, taking risks, maturity, growing up, letting go... Need I go on?

Reflections is a yawner tonight. Bob has been under the weather lately, and doesn't seem bent on his usual digging for more emotional release from patients. He doesn't even take role call before we start, failing to notice that Angel of Death Girl is missing.

"Okay, who's next?" he says, his eyes half shut. It sounds like his nose is pinched shut with a clothespin. "That's nice, Stanley. Thank you. Are we finally to the end? Oh, that's right. We have Gary yet. Didn't you share twice last night?"

"Well, I—"

"I thought so. If that's the case, and since you've been doing so well lately, why don't we call it a night? Oh wait, is it movie night?" He sighs, his nose red and puffy. It almost looks like he uses sandpaper for a hanky. "Okay, I'll get Ariel down here to pop the corn and set it up. If you'll excuse me, I need to—"

He hustles down the corridor sneezing and blowing his nose like a bugle.

The rest of us get up and disperse to nightly routines. Some watch TV until the movie is set up, many pluck cigarettes from their shirt pockets and duck into the smoking room, and still others sit around and chew the fat while waiting for the featured flick to start. Tonight's showing: *Gone With the Wind*. A few of the older crowd swoon with excitement. I've never heard of it. Does it have to do with tornados?

Since it's not mandatory to watch the movie, I decide to go to my room and write in my journal. I'm getting seriously hooked on writing. It's part of my addictive personality I think. I discovered this yesterday while talking with Ariel. She gave me the assignment in Assertiveness Class to diagram out genuine interests and talents I may have, beliefs I stand for, and what I sincerely aspire to do with my life. My list thus far:

Possible Careers	Interests	Beliefs
1) Doctor	*1) Reading*	*1) I am stubborn, but it's okay*
2) Counselor	*2) Writing*	*2) Life is bigger than me*
3) Writer	*3) Watching movies*	*3) Happiness is not things*
4) Dietician	*4) Music*	*4) People are not perfect*
5) Teacher	*5) Theater/acting*	*5) God is not a policeman*

Push-ups and sit-ups are waiting, remember? Feel the bubbling in your fat cells?

I don't know. Is this constant burden to rid calories and obsess over a weight number really worth it?

Why do you even question any other option? There's something seriously wrong with you lately.

You're maturing and changing, that's what.

All is quiet as I meditate on these last words from YOU.

Ariel barges into my room. "C'mon, Gary. Why don't you sit and watch this movie? It's a classic. It'd be good for you."

"Sorry. I don't really care to. I'm rather tired and I'd like to go do some journaling before bed."

How can she say no to journaling?

"You can journal all day if you want. Sit and enjoy the company for a while. Take your socks off. Relax. You don't need to be productive all the time. Be lazy—"

"Okay, okay," I say in exasperation, throwing my hands into the air. "I catch your drift. I'll watch for a little while."

"That's the spirit. Why don't you help me get the popcorn ready."

We pop three bags of heavily buttered popcorn and almost short out the popping machine. I request a bag without butter. Coffee cups are distributed to hold the popcorn. The VCR is set. Cigarettes are extinguished. The lights go down. Showtime. Five minutes into the opening credits, I'm almost asleep. It doesn't take me long to figure out this ancient production has nothing to do with tornadoes.

"Wow," *sniff,* exclaims Hadie, "just look at those beautiful dresses. Don't you reckon they sweated like pigs wearing those suffocating buttresses and frilly gowns all day?" *Sniff.* "Not for me, I'll tell you...." *Sniff.* She scoops a cup full of popcorn and disappears up the dimmed corridor. Ariel left about a minute earlier to do charting.

I better ditch now before the usher comes back.

As I saunter back up the corridor past the dining hall, I hear crying and whimpering to my left. I see no one at first, but upon following the sniffling sound trail, I notice Angel of Death Girl huddled in a corner by the window. She is tightly curled in a chair behind a small table she obviously pulled behind a rubber tree plant. Her wrist is wrapped with heavy gauze bandage. A Styrofoam bowl of Froot Loops under her chin catches a flow of tears. She dangles a spoon, pushing the rainbow rings back and forth across a pond of milk. At first, I question whether or not I should investigate. But my heart slides down onto my sleeve, and my gut cries out for me to do something.

Take another risk. Comfort her.

Without scrutinizing the moment further, I slowly ease my way over to her table.

"May I sit down?" I ask. She doesn't say a word. I take that as a yes. "What's the matter?"

Long, black, oily hair droops over her flushed cheeks. No answer. Tears let up. I sit quietly to illicit possible after effects, but nothing.

Okay, then... I push my chair out to get up and leave. "I'm sorry, uh... I never got your name, but I'll leave you in—"

"Em," mumbles the girl.

"I'm sorry, but I didn't understand—"

"Emilee," blurts the girl. "My name is Emilee." She heaves a full breath of air and exhales slowly, blowing some hair away from her face. She tucks the leftovers behind her ears.

Never in my life have I seen such a beautiful face. Her fine, smooth skin with high cheekbones—wet and streaked with eyeliner—glow in the pale fluorescent lighting of the dining hall. Deep, dark, gorgeous brown eyes look saddened and empty.

I stagger onward. "How did you...? How come you're...? What happened?"

"I don't know," she snivels. Her voice is sweet and mild.

"That's okay," I say. "You don't have to talk about it if—"

"No, that's not what I meant. What I meant was, well, I don't know if I can talk about it."

I stare at her in silence, waiting. Her eyes catch another look at me, wondering, hoping, debating...?

"I don't want to be here," she says. Her lips squeeze together. "I can't stand it anymore."

"I know how it is. This unit can get pretty—"

She shakes her head briskly. "No, it's not the unit. It's that I don't want to be here—living in life anymore. There's no point to it whatsoever, no meaning behind the façades. Why did it all have to happen to me? Why am I so bad?"

I don't know what to do. Somehow, I believe words would just get in the way. I find myself wanting to hold her hand, to give her a hug, but that doesn't seem appropriate, either. I don't have to wait any longer.

"Ever since I was five, all I wanted to do was dance. I loved it," she says with a slight whimper. The few Froot Loops left floating in her bowl have soaked up so much milk that they've ballooned to the size of nickels. "Mom put me through years of ballet, and I couldn't think of anyone who could be happier than me. Years went by, even though mom and dad would argue—when Dad was home...and drinking. He's gone a lot on business, you know. But when I was in seventh grade, things began to change for the worse." Her face tightens. She begins twirling a lock of her hair. "My body started growing in a way that I didn't want it to grow—in a girl way, you know. At first I liked it. I had lots of boyfriends and attention, which felt good. Pretty soon, Dad would start yelling at me to kick my leg higher or practice harder. Mom got on my case about getting a B in chemistry—the first B in my life. I just couldn't seem to please them enough, you know, no matter how many awards I won..."

She pauses to caress the heavy gauze wrapped around her wrist.

My heart beats forcefully, rattling my chest bones. Her last words sent a strange vibe down my spine. I don't ask.

She continues as if reliving a horrible scene all over again, her voice trembling. "Then, a couple years ago, Dad came home drunk. Mom was out chaperoning a birthday party that my little brother went to. I had just taken my shower and put on my pajamas to sit and watch some TV, when Dad came staggering into the room yelling and swearing at me. He ordered me up to my room and switched the channel to a football game. I took off for my room, slammed the door shut, put a pillow over my head, and cried because I was terrified—because I know what he was capable of... I tried not to think about it, but only minutes later, sure enough, he was standing right over me. He—"

Ariel walks by the dining hall and sees us talking. We both look at her and freeze. Emilee does her best to stifle a full blown breakdown. Ariel pauses for a second, smiles, and then keeps walking past to the lounge, popcorn cup in hand.

Emilee's tears begin to flow.

I try to save her. "Emilee, you don't have to go any further if you—"

She waves me off, talking through the tears. "He put his hand on my back and began to rub. I didn't move, just clenched my sheets in my mouth. He liked to do this a lot. He told me he was giving me a massage, that he liked how I was maturing into a pretty young lady, that he... he..."

I run over to the coffee pot table, snatch a pile of napkins, and lay them in front of her. The sobbing intensifies, her forearm sopping with wiped tears. She doesn't touch the napkins.

"He began yelling at me, saying I was worthless and lazy. I covered my head with my pillow, but he ripped it out of my hands and began kicking me, slapping me." She swats her hand in the air and kicks the chair next to me, her eyes large and focused straight ahead, as if giving a play-by-play while watching the heart-wrenching scene on a TV screen in front of her. "I ran out of the room, out the front door, and down the street to a playground. I sat for most of the night on the swings crying, waiting until my father was finally passed out on the couch for the evening, like usual."

I'm dumbfounded about what to say next. She finally concedes to wiping her eyes and blemish-free face with a fistful of napkins and blows her immaculately formed nose. Matted strands of her hair fight to hang back over her brow. Emilee swings them out of her way.

"Then a couple months ago, I began dating this guy. He was so sweet and accepted me for me. He always behaved like a perfect gentleman, no matter how much trouble he got into. I tried to make him happy, and it worked for a while. I even started to dress like him, even though Mom freaked when I went Goth. But things changed, like they always do." She takes a shaky breath. "Last month, while watching a movie at his house in the basement, he started acting all weird. He'd...he'd...he'd put his hand on my butt and...and then... He reached inside my—I wanted to please him... I was terrified that he might hurt me—even worse than my Dad hurt Mom... I wanted someone to love me so badly, without any strings, like he told me he did so many times before... Then he...he..." She firmly twists and intertwines her fingers, her hands engaged in one vehement tremor. "... he... he touched me. I pushed him away and told him I wasn't that kind of a girl. Then he said, 'Yes, you are,' and he threw me down on the floor. I was scared and didn't know what to do. He pulled off my pants and...did it. I...I...wanted to fall right through the floor and disappear, never to return again. I wanted him to die! But he said he loved me, the one who came to every one of my dance recitals, gave me flowers, told me I was beautiful and talented. I couldn't let him down." Emilee looks up at the ceiling, sniffling, her eyes swollen and teary. "He told me if I ever told anyone he'd kill me. But I couldn't take it anymore. I'm such a terrible person for saying this, but I wanted to die. Mom found me in the bathtub with a razor in my hand. I hate my body. I hate my wretched life. It caused all this mess. Why did my body have to change? If I'd only made my parents happier, gotten even better grades maybe, then they wouldn't fight, then none of this would have happened."

Emilee buries her face in her hands, sobbing. I feel useless, though I'd give a million dollars to take her pain away.

"What an awful experience you've been through," I say, gently patting her shoulder. She flinches at first but doesn't pull away.

After a few minutes of unrestrained weeping, she lifts her head and blows her nose. "Yeah."

Now what do I do? My problems pale miserably in comparison to what she's been through.

"Thanks, Gary, for listening to me." She sniffs heavily, blowing her nose yet again and tossing the Kleenex on the mound of others next to her. "I've never told this stuff to anyone before, not even with Arty in group. I can tell he knows something about me, but I'm not comfortable talking to him right now."

"Hey, I know that feeling," I admit. "I despised the guy at first during my last hospital visit, but he got tears out of me that I was too stubborn to let free. He was good that way."

"I'm scared, Gary. What do I do? What if Mark finds out I ratted on him? He said he'd kill me."

I don't know what to say. After a brief bout of crying, Emilee blows her nose again and takes a deep breath.

"Well, anyhow, enough about me. How are things going with you?"

Never in my life have I been more eager to answer a question than at this very moment. For the next hour, I share with Emilee my entire life story, including something that few ears have heard up to this point.

"Emilee, I know how awful people can be sometimes..." I want to talk to her. I want to tell her stuff I never talk about.

She wipes some last tears, and looks right at me. She *wants* me to talk to her.

"During my elementary years, this guy Mark Ponchkin had been the biggest neighborhood bully to me. Of course, around adults, he could be the nicest kid when he wanted to be. But when the teachers were chatting and not watching us, he and his friends were such jerks. He'd dump milk on me at lunch, trip me in the hall, and push books out of my arms. I never said anything because I knew if I told anyone, he'd probably make it worse. No one would believe me, either."

Emilee's nodding as I talk, listening to every word.

It feels so good to unload this story to someone. "Then, when I was in fifth grade, I was waiting for my mom after basketball practice. I knew Mark was always jealous of me because I held my own against him in sports. I was waiting alone, under an awning to stay out of the rain. His cronies jumped me when I wasn't looking, dragged me out onto the wet lawn, and held me face down. Mark stepped on the back of my head and squashed it hard into the grass. I couldn't breathe because my nostrils were stuffed with something that made me gag. It smelled like dog poop. He grabbed my hair, yanked my head back, and rammed in hard into the ground. I tried to wiggle free but it was no use. Someone clucked like a chicken and kicked me hard between the legs and yelled 'Stupid chicken!' The pain was unbearable. I had no choice. What was most humiliating was how hard they all laughed when I told them I thought it tasted good, just to try and please them so they would leave me alone. It was pathetic, I was so wimpy." I feel sick again just remembering it. "They kicked me around some more before they stuffed dirty, wet grass down my throat, which made me throw up *yet again*. They left me in the mud, wet and cold and smeared with dog poop."

"God, that's horrible," Emilee says.

"Yeah, and then Mom yelled at me for how dirty my clothes were when she picked me up. I told her me and a couple friends were wrestling for fun, and it got out of hand. I never showed her my black and blue ribs, or my swollen groin. I told her my black eye was from ramming into a tree. For years after that, Mark teased and threatened me constantly without anyone knowing. He'd sometimes even steal my homework or tear it up only an hour before it was due. He told me I'd hurt a lot worse if I ever told anyone anything."

I can count all of Emilee's teeth. Her mouth is wide open. I see no tables or rubber tree plants, no psychiatric unit, no staff. We are the only two people in the room. I suddenly feel very, very free. The time races by all too quickly.

"You know," I continue, "it just amazes me that someone so successful and pretty as you would choose to do something like—"

Then it hits me between the eyes like a brick.

"Like what?" says Emilee.

After a moment of intense contemplation, I say, "I think the answer just came to me."

"What do you mean?"

"You and I—we're almost exactly alike in that way." The gears in my mind are still twisting and whirring with revelation. I'm flabbergasted that I didn't see it before. "It's funny, we're both talented teenagers with lots of potential, but somehow it's so much easier to spot in someone else and not ourselves."

"Ah-Ah-Ah-Ah-*chooooooo*!" sneezes Bob, cutting in on us. "Time for bed you two. Did you have a good visit?" He blows his nose like a foghorn.

"Yeah," we say together. Emilee reaches out her arms, inviting me in for a hug. Not even a tornado from *Gone with the Wind* could have kept me from obliging.

CHAPTER THIRTY-FIVE

BUSTED

*G*et off your fatty rear-end.
Sorry, I don't particularly care to. I'm flying high on Emilee right now.

You're going to feel flabby in the morning if you don't.

I know, but—

Get out your journal.

No buts. Just do it.

Where's my journal. Oh, here it is... *Dear God, I—*

Bob is pulling graveyard shift tonight, sick. He's doing rounds every other hour tonight. People have gone to sleep. Your muscles need soreness.

Focus on what you want to do, not what the eating disorder wants.

You're simply being selfish and lazy.

You're being responsible.

Lazy.

Responsible.

I try to keep writing. *Dear God, I feel like I'm being stretched between two—*

Super lazy.

Super responsible.

You're getting cold feet, Gary, and for good reason. If you avoid my help now, you won't know what to do with yourself.

Don't listen to—

You'll feel guilty and won't be able to handle life on your own. Admit it—you need me. Life is just too darn stressful, too many people to please, too many expectations to live up to.

Pick, pick, pick...

My journal page corners sharply dig under my thumbnail—I can't shake this nervous habit. Things really are going sort of fast for me lately. Maybe I—

Feeling uncomfortable and out-of-the-box is normal. Focus beyond the feeling and concentrate on your capability. Feelings can be fickle. They're—

—avoidable in your life. Why feel them and cause yourself so much grief?

Pick, pick, pick...

Listen to me.

No, listen to *me*. You can—

—kiss your comfortability and control good-bye if you don't heed my warning.

Focus—

—on me!

No, me!

PICK, PICK, PICK... I dig the page of my journal so far under my thumbnail that blood forms. I feel like I just struck oil. Out of frustration, I tear out a journal page and shred it, pitching the pieces at the trashcan. Most pieces miss and haphazardly flutter to the floor.

Don't think. Just do.

But that's my saying—

Do it. Now. A little workout isn't going to hurt you, anyhow. You can do whatever you want later.

You're right. What the heck. Let's go.

You're a Navy SEAL, a Green Beret...

Down to the floor I flop. "One, two, three, four..." One hundred push-ups are counted out to my humming cadence of "The Ballad of the Green Berets." My arms go numb. They feel like spaghetti.

Running in place... Go!

Kneecaps flail. I've never kicked them so high before in my life. I'm kicking with such force that my left knee thwacks me in the chin. My tongue is in the wrong place at the wrong time. Blood coats my teeth. Three minutes later, I hoist myself into my bed. "One... two... three..." Sit-ups are executed with precise tightening of specific muscles around my abdominal cavity. "... fifty-three... fifty-four...."

What am I doing? I'm wasting my parents' hard-earned money. Why do I cheat them like this?

Selfish brute.

But you keep telling me—

It's your own fault. Think of how they'll feel, the sadness and desperation, the lost hope in what could be for you. What a waste of great potential you've turned out to be.

"... one hundred fifteen... one hundred sixteen..." A vertebrae in my back cracks, sending shooting searing pain down my legs. "Ouch... one hundred twenty-two..." *Huff, huff...* "One hundred twenty-three..." *Huff, huff...*

Dizziness sets in, blurring my vision. Blood tastes like warm steel. How many calories?

Keep going! You must keep—

"Gary?" emerges a soft voice from a smidgen of light glaring in from the doorway. I stop in mid-push. "You forgot to get your amitriptyline. I figured I'd bring it to— What are you doing?" Bob looks like a zombie with a balding scalp.

Huuuuuff, huuuuuff, huuuuuff, huuuuuff...

I freeze, trying with all my might to reduce my rapid panting.

"Gary, are you feeling anxious right now?" He enters and closes the door to a crack. The end of my bed sags down from his nasally girth. "Well? How are you feeling right now?"

Huuuuuff, huuuuuff, huuuuff...

"It's important for you when you're feeling anxious to seek out staff to talk. How come you chose otherw—Ah-Ah-Ah-Ah-Ah-*choooooooooo*!"

Swallow your pride. It's okay. There's no indignity in acceptance.

Yes, there—

"You're right, Bob." He *is* right, and I'm frustrated. "You're right, I should have sought you out..."

You should have—the story of your life.

"... but I didn't. I'm sorry."

Bob empathizes. "There's no need to apologize."

"But I can control it. Really, I can."

"Gary... Think about it."

"I'm tired of thinking about it. I'm tired of fighting this nagging eating disorder. I'm tired of always feeling like I must exercise. I can't take this anymore. I can't, I can't, I can't!"

"Then don't," replies Bob candidly. "Don't take it anymore."

Anger grabs hold of my voice. "What do you mean don't take it anymore?" I say tersely.

The words explode from my lips before I have a chance to take control. I can't believe I'm actually showing anger to someone else.

You're in trouble now, buster.

"Let go. Give in. Surrender," says Bob without a change in expression, completely unfazed by my outburst.

"But how do—?"

"You're doing it right now. You're giving in to the temptation to stuff all your embarrassed, hurt, guilty feelings..."

You're making a choice.

"... you're making a choice to do so—to let go of your feelings."

We sit and talk for another half hour. Relief bubbles within my core, weakening my eyelids. I feel relaxed, content from talking with Bob, and now taking advantage of the rest found in a warm, inviting bed.

Set the alarm for 4:00 a.m.

Hold up your white flag.

You win. You win. I give up. I want to let go of you.

YOU?

No, you—as in IT, you stupid voice.

What did you—

Jim Gantner has a good strategy. Mocking can work.

No, it can't.

You know, your barking is getting really old. If that's all the better you can do, you stupid eating disorder... Oh, what's the use? The heck with it...

Keep going.

I'm sorry, YOU, but I'm just so tired.

My eyes shut. No alarm is set. My heart turns over to beat quietly to a different drummer. I let go to sleep.

CHAPTER THIRTY-SIX

ARIEL'S LESSONS: GIRLS 101

Jezi turns off the power to her electric pottery wheel today. She continues to stick religiously to her flighty ways. Most days, she surprises us patients with the newest in bead design, wood carving, plaster mold construction, needle point patterns, or a host of other projects that happen to tickle her fancy over bagels and juice that morning.

Today, a box of doughnuts sits open in the center of the work table.

"Grab a doughnut," say Jezi. "They're on me. Then find a seat where you can get relaxed and comfortable."

Stanley wanders aimlessly around the room. His nostrils twitch and flare slightly at the smell of the donuts, temporarily taking his attention away from his constant project to button the cuffs on his shirt. An elderly male patient with a bald head like a potato follows Stanley into the room like a trained collie. He's stout and hunched over, looking a lot like Igor the food-cart pusher. Something stringy and white dangles in his hand.

"Stanley, why don't you and Floyd sit on chairs over—Stanley! It's time to give your cufflink buttoning assignment a rest. Plant yourself. You can sit on the floor, lay on the table, curl up on the window sill, I don't care. Just get someplace where you can relax and—Floyd!"

Jezi snatches the cloth object from Floyd's grasp. "Where did you get this bra?" Floyd's age shows. It takes him a few seconds for his brain to react to Jezi. His leathery head slowly turns toward Jezi with a surprised look.

The group erupts in gut-busting laughter. It feels good to laugh. The chuckling tenses my stomach muscles.

I look around for Emilee but see her nowhere. "Jezi? Where's Emilee?"

"Her doctor hasn't ordered O.T. for her." Jezi grabs the box of doughnuts off the table. "Here, Gary, have one."

Never snack between meals. It adds fat.

One doughnut will not hurt you.

"No thanks," I decline politely.

Jezi decides to keep going. "C'mon, Gary. It's just a little doughnut. It won't hurt you."

"Honest, I don't care for any. I'm still full from lunch."

"Can I have his?" asks Stanley, eagerly sniffing toward the doughnuts.

Jezi remains focused on me. "No, Stanley." She shoves the box under my chin. I gently push it away, smiling at her. She rattles the box. I look down at my shoes. She grabs a napkin and pinches a chocolate covered doughnut with sprinkles, laying it in my lap.

"Just in case you change your mind," she says, and moves on to Floyd, who ignores the doughnuts but instead works on recapturing the bra still hanging from Jezi's hand. I toss the doughnut aside. It lands frosting down into a small dust hill, sprinkles scattering everywhere.

Jezi explains the task as she positions a small tape recorder next to her that she pulled from the back storage room. "We're going to be doing a relaxation exercise today. You're going to hear a tape of tranquil nature sounds. A guy with a soothing voice is going to be giving you directions to tighten and relax specific muscles in your body. Just find the most relaxing position possible and go with the flow of the tape. Everyone ready? Okay, go ahead and shut your eyes, and here we go..." She turns on the tape recorder and adjusts the volume. "No peeking now."

Tinkling crystals with an ocean wave background begins to play over two small speakers attached to a run-down portable eight-track/cassette-tape player. I sit on the floor with my legs stretched out and my palms up on my lap. My eyelids close for a while. Five minutes into the tape, Stanley snores like a chainsaw. The serene baritone voice on the tape doesn't care.

"... Now let's ease our boat into shore from the peaceful, clear blue waters. The pull to shore feels sensitive to your feet and fatigued arms from rowing..." *Tinkle, tinkle, tinkle...*

Stanley: *Zzzzzzzzz...*

Someone tip Stanley's canoe. I can't get rested to get to shore.

We tighten our eyes...relax, tighten our necks...relax, tighten our shoulders...relax, tighten our arms...relax, all the way down to our toes and back. It's a long journey, but one that finds me feeling like a jellyfish in the middle of the Pacific with sunbeams glinting through the silent waters.

Your body deserves this type of rest. It's okay to experience.

No, it isn't.

Well, I can't deny that I certainly like it. We all walk back to the unit with our bodies feeling incredibly tranquil and rejuvenated. I want to go back to the beach with fine, warm, tropical sand.

Floyd trudges behind Stanley, clasping the front of his shirt as if he's having a heart attack. At first I'm alarmed, but then I notice a bra strap poking out from the bottom of Floyd's shirt. I should hire the man to work for me hiding food at the dinner table.

When I get back to my room, I see a folded piece of paper resting upon a freshly made bed. Housekeeping is great. I wish they'd do my chores at home, even though Mom and Dad don't give me many. They've been content with doing most things themselves to save time and bickering.

The note has my name on it. I open it quickly:

Dear Gary,

How are you? I'm doing much better since our talk last night. Thanks again for taking the time to sit and listen to my problems. I don't have many friends right now—that is, that I can trust. You were the first person I ever really talked to about my father or Mark. I can't talk to my mom anymore. I've tried, but she doesn't believe me. I'm afraid to tell the police because I don't want anything bad to happen to my dad. He hurts me, but I still love him and don't want him to get taken away. It would put my mother over the edge, and it would be all my fault.

Anyway, I was wondering if you'd like to take a walk with me sometime, on a pass or something. Please write back, or tell me in person. Talk to you later. —Em

I have no clue where the idea came from, but my heart began to pump madly at the thought of it. With note still in hand, I went to hunt for Emilee. I found her in the laundry room helping a frail old woman transfer wet, heavy clothes from the washer to the dryer.

My words weren't exactly poetry, but it did the trick, I guess. "Ah, excuse me, Em? Would, uh... you, uh...you know, sort of, like... want to, uh... eat me tonight—I mean eat with me tonight?"

Pathetic.

She doesn't seem to care that I sounded like a total dork. "Oh, Gary, that's a great idea. How fun."

The truth hits me hard. I have no practical dating experience with girls beyond this point, even though I've dreamed of this moment for years. I thought it would never come to pass. What do I do? Do I hold her hand? Buy her a plant or something? I'll have to seriously consider the possibilities. It's quite a risk being with a girl, though I've been getting lots of practice with risk taking lately. Each time I've done it so far, I've been pleased with the results. It's not as earth-shatteringly painful as IT —I mean my eating disorder— tells me.

I approach Hadie the next day with my idea, and to my utmost relief, I don't have a problem convincing her to let Emilee come along. In fact, she loved the plan. It fits perfectly into the staff's goals for me to socialize and build healthy communication skills. However, Atalanta exhibits firm disagreement with the idea. She thinks it will only detract from my focus. She probably didn't get a date for her prom.

The only catch is that someone would need to supervise the entire evening. I pick Ariel. The weather for tonight: a chilly, clear evening, with a chance of light snow flurries. Sounds good so far.

The clock ticks away slowly all day, like someone shut off time. Lunch isn't here yet? Group therapy actually zips past because I'm a little chatterbox, powered with Emilee electricity. My eating disorder is barely a whisper. She and I sit side-by-side, throwing smiles at each other every minute or so.

After a quick bite to eat for lunch, which I have minor issues consuming, I fill up ten pages in my journal. My dialogue has nothing to do with the macaroni and cheese I just ate, or fat feelings, or worrying about not feeling hungry enough after my next meal. It's all Emilee this and Emilee that, every other sentence starting with "Emilee."

Atalanta does some kind of affirmations class before O.T. We give ourselves hugs and create personal billboards of positive messages we can saturate our minds with throughout the day. My sign reads, "I am a worthwhile human being," "Emilee is cool," "I am capable," "Emilee is awesome," "I am deserving of others' help," "Emilee is beautiful." What's the matter with that clock? I want to grab a ladder, climb up to it, and push the hands forward about three hours.

O.T. has us back to molding pottery. My goal is to construct a vase for Emilee and fill it with wildflowers, but my anti-artsy disease has me starting over six times without any luck. The closest I come to a vase is a lopsided ashtray. Flowers won't fit in an ashtray. I guess I'll have to buy her something from the gift shop instead. Maybe I could call Mom and have her bring me up something from last spring's inventory I have stockpiled in my closet. Too tacky. I wish I could ask someone about this dating stuff. I try Ariel.

"Now, make sure you open doors for her and don't forget to pull out her chair before she sits down," explains Ariel who's more than happy to educate me on the finer points of dating etiquette with girls.

I looked confused. "Pull out her chair before she sits? But won't that be rude? She'll drop to the ground."

"Not as she's ready to sit down, you dope," says Ariel, rolling her eyes, "although I'd love to see how she'd react to that one. No, you pull the chair out for her to sit on, then assist her up to the table." She demonstrates with me using one of the dining room chairs.

"While you eat, you're going to have to talk to her, too. This is usually hard to do for guys. I'm not talking about mushy stuff. Ask about how things are going for her at school. Inquire about her interests, her hopes, her dreams. Just be honest about what's going through that little head of yours and be yourself."

The more Ariel talks, the more I feel this is going to be an insurmountable task.

You'll fail miserably for sure. Once she sees past your fakeness, she'll brush you off like a fly on her nose.

"And don't be in such a great hurry to be affectionate, although I don't think this will be an issue with you. Let her warm up to you at her pace. Follow her lead, and do only what you sense she's willing to allow."

"I guess I'm not following you," I say, scratching my head.

"Okay, let me show you." She positions my body shoulder to shoulder with hers. "Let's say we're taking a walk together."

We begin to walk around the tables, her shoulders nonchalantly rubbing up against mine. I shy away, taken aback by the weird feeling of an older woman touching me.

"Whoa, where're you going?" asks Ariel, tugging me back to her side. "Rule number one: If she stays close, you stay close. If she gently collides with your shoulder, it's probably a sign that she feels comfortable with you. In other words, stay close and follow her lead. But be gentle. Don't bop her"—she slams her shoulder into mine like a halfback bouncing off a defender, sending me flopping on top of a table— "like that. Oops! I don't know my own strength."

I push myself erect and smile. "Yeah, right," I say lightheartedly. "Sure you don't."

She continues showing me a few other tricks of the trade, like when and how to hold her hand ("You softly caress it in your palm, not squeezing it like an orange to make juice") and how to kiss: "You press limply but tenderly on her lips, like this." She demonstrates by pressing her lips against the back of her hand and makes wet slurping noises, like she's overstuffed her mouth with Jell-O. "Actually, it's probably best you wait on this one. Maybe follow her lead. Girls can be funny sometimes; she might think you're only after sex—"

"*WHAT?*"

Ariel nearly jumps out of her shoes. "Well, I didn't mean it like *that*," she says with a self-conscious smirk, and watching me turn such a bright shade of red that my head could pass for a ripe strawberry.

"It's just that you're better off catering to her soft, romantic side first and if she's ready to...to...oh, never mind. That's an advanced lesson all on its own."

She looked at the floor, paused... then blurted, "Look, if you want to kiss her, I suggest you politely ask her first. It may feel a little embarrassing, but she'll respect you for it. If she says no, take it in good stride and say, 'I appreciate you telling me. I really like you, Emilee, and hope to continue our relationship, and wouldn't want to do anything to jeopardize that."

Ariel decides I've had enough girl lessons for today, but finishes with a few last reminders, such as never making vulgar noises that originate from any body part whatsoever.

I never realized how inept I am with these techniques that probably come naturally to most teenagers. This is already shaping up to be a night I'll never forget.

CHAPTER THIRTY-SEVEN

THE ELEVATOR RIDE TO HEAVEN

Dinnertime finally arrives. I'm not the least bit hungry, being a tight ball of nerves, though it's a pleasant sort of nervous. Okay... breathe...relax... I'm floating to shore in a canoe upon gently rippling waters... *Tinkle, tinkle, tinkle...* I think I'm going to go tinkle in my pants.

Emilee emerges from her room at the far end of the hallway. There's a swooping feeling in my stomach that I don't particularly want to disappear. Her greasy hair has disappeared, as it's tied back into a springy, silky ponytail. She's also treated herself to some light makeup, which gives her the appearance of someone on the cover of a magazine. She seems to be radiating heat.

You dirty pervert.

No, don't bother me, not right now.

Forget your eating disorder. Enjoy the moment. You have my permission.

"Ready, you two?" says Ariel, giving me a wink. She allows us to make the journey by ourselves while she straggles two horse lengths behind. A fiesta of multicolored, blinking lights hanging from the ceiling greets us upon arrival to the cafeteria. Green and red garlands decorate the salad bar counters and twist around support beams. Nat King Cole is piped in, singing "White Christmas" over the sound system. The season is in full swing, a perfect evening. Tonight's menu, an in-season special: St. Nick Steak and Baked Potato with Tinsel Garnish, Stocking Stuffer Mixed Veggies, and Ho-Ho Bread Pudding.

One of the Beefy Bertha partners greets me with a jolly hello. "Well, well, Gary, entertaining guests this evening, are we?"

The other half takes notice. "And such a pretty young lass, too?" She points above our heads. Mistletoe dangles.

Emilee and I blush.

Somehow, I get the feeling that prom would have been like this. I slide my tray through the line, intent on choosing whatever Emilee decides to take, which is slim pickings: a plain baked potato, raspberry yogurt, and water. The urge to impress her comes over me. I order the works: steak and potato, double mixed veggies, bread pudding, salad bar, ice cream cup, and chocolate milk.

Oink, oink.

Ignore it. Stay focused on Emilee.

No worries. I don't need to eat it all anyhow.

Ariel generously offers to take care of the bill so I can lead Emilee to my regular cozy table in the corner. I start by pulling out her chair, just like Ariel taught me.

"What a gentleman," says Emilee.

I look over at Ariel, who grins and gives me a thumbs up before taking a seat next to a slew of hospital workers with floppy blue gowns and little blue booties.

The first five minutes is taken up with lots of chewing. I begin to regret ever wanting to impress Emilee by stacking my tray with enough food for the both of us. My fork picks and pokes away at my baked potato while she quietly eats her yogurt. Every now and then we come up for air to smile at each other; however, the silence soon begins to take its toll on my nerves. I wish she'd say something. I shift in my chair and cough. I glance over at Ariel, who just happens to be looking over her shoulder at us. She shakes her head with a grin and tries mouthing words silently to me, but I have no clue as to what they are. Something about caulk or balk or hawk, I don't know. I mouth the word "what?" right back at her, hopefully to get clarification. But it's no use. I have no idea what she—

"Is everything okay?" asks Emilee, startling me back to attention.

"Uh, yeah, I was just waving at someone I knew." I mentally dig into my mind in an endeavor to pull out mental notes from Ariel's Girls 101 crash course, but it's no use. I find nothing but cobwebs.

"This is nice, just you and me," says Emilee, prying open her baked potato.

"Yeah, it is."

You are hopeless.

No you're not. Remember what Ariel talked about; just be honest with what's going on inside your head.

"Uh, Emilee," I cough out before my fear has a chance to paralyze my mouth shut, "I, uh, I guess I'm a little, well, nervous and all and, well, what I mean is being around a pretty girl like you makes..."

A vibrant, rosy smile stretches across Emilee's beautifully smooth face. "Oh, Gary..." she mutters shyly, looking back down at her tray.

Oh, great. Now I probably embarrassed her too much. Now she'll never want to—

"You know, I was feeling the same way myself," smiles Emily. She's leaning upright on her elbows and looking a bit more relaxed than a few seconds ago.

I'm feeling more relaxed now, too, almost like there's warm water being poured over my body, melting away the icy tension.

For the rest of the meal, we talk about everything under the sun, from favorite movies to summer jobs. We look into each other's eyes more freely and laugh at each other's attempts at humor. I don't try to impress her by playing a mental round of Let's Be Somebody Else.

You see, Ariel was right. It pays to take a risk every now and again, doesn't it?

I can't argue with you there.

I suddenly become aware that half of my steak and nearly all of my baked potato have disappeared. This scares me at first, but enjoying Emilee's company has reduced the anxiety I usually endure during a meal. Since Emilee has finished eating, I decide to call it quits myself and leave the rest of my food untouched. My nerves spring to life again as we depart the cafeteria. I'm uncertain about what's ahead, but I wouldn't trade this nervousness for a trillion dollars.

We bid Ariel good night as we put on our winter coats to get ready for our walk. "Enjoy your time, you two," says Ariel, stacking our cluttered trays on top of hers, "but I need you to be back to the unit in about an hour, okay?"

The time has arrived. The walk.

The air is nippy, the sky is opaque, making it brighter than a blanket of stars, and a gentle snow speckles our hatless heads, giving us the look of major dandruff. We stroll along the many winding, shoveled pathways of the hospital courtyard, our hands swinging slowly side by side with fingers conveniently bumping into one another.

"What a perfect winter evening, isn't it, Gary?"

I'm intoxicated with strange feelings. "Yeah, it is...perfect."

Emilee draws her stride closer to mine to where our shoulders rub together. Our fingers softly intertwine. She nestles my hand within both of hers and gives it a tender pat.

Heaven. That's all I can say. My stomach dips and dives with all the exhilaration of a roller coaster. Never in my life have I felt such a rush of unusual feelings, but they're pure ecstasy. I could endure a root canal at this moment without Novocain.

"You know, Gary, ever since we've opened up to each other, I can't help but think how close we've become. I think our hospital experience has taken us to a deeper level than other people could ever know. What do you think?"

I nod robustly. "Yeah, I agree."

"It's hard to imagine that all of this is happening so fast. What do you think?"

"Yeah, I agree."

Emilee could literally get me to agree to absolutely anything right now. My intense infatuation with her seems illogical, unreal, and too good to be true for me.

It is.

I am so sick of you.

Me?

No, not YOU... I mean—you know, I don't want to bother with my eating disorder anymore. I'm missing out on far too much life. The time is ripe. It's time.

What do you mean?

I can hardly believe all this has suddenly been placed in my lap, sort of like winning a jackpot I didn't even know I signed up for. I don't want to explore the tiny notion inside me that says this will all end soon, that a girl of this beauty who I feel such an intense pull of attraction toward could ever in a million years entertain interest in a desperate, inexperienced, insecure guy like me.

You deserve every enchanted feeling of this evening. Don't allow your eating disorder to spoil it. Keep focused on me.

We make three revolutions of the hospital grounds and take a break. I brush snow off a pathway bench as we settle in close together. Emilee rests her head on my shoulder and pulls my arm around her neck. Ariel's voice materializes in my mind: "...just let her lead..."

Good. I can do this. I follow and take notes.

I sit in silence for a while, engrossed in her soft, fruity-smelling hair resting against the side of my face. I feel older and more confident, like I'm the man of the house and our children are home with a babysitter. I watch her breath slowly expelling in mild puffs. It smells of raspberry yogurt, which has now suddenly become my all-time favorite flavor. I glance at my watch. Forty-five minutes have elapsed.

Already?

It's time to head in. We get inside the hospital front entrance and stop at the gift shop. I purchase Emilee a rose.

"Oh, Gary, how totally romantic," swoons Emilee, looking at the flower as if it were a newborn kitten.

Wow, I think I scored again. I could get used to this dating stuff.

We walk hand in hand to the double elevators. Emilee pushes the "up" button, and immediately a young family carrying a bouquet of "Get Well" balloons comes filtering out, with two people remaining inside. I start forward to get in, but Emilee tugs me back.

"Let's wait for the next one," she says matter-of-factly.

No argument here. Something seems fishy, though.

Within seconds, the other elevator door slides open. An elderly gentleman with a walker slowly rolls over the threshold and putts away. Emilee takes a quick peek inside: It's empty. She leads us forward, letting go of my hand to punch the button for the third floor. She rests herself against the back railing. I follow her lead, like I've been doing the whole evening. The doors shut. Emilee's fingers crawl over mine on the railing, sending warm jolts of energy through my body. We look at each other and smile, trying to read each other's minds.

"Uh, Emilee..." I stammer. "Do you, uh, well... do you want to, uh..."

Emilee looks at me expectantly.

"Do you want to—"

Ooof! Mmmm. Mmmmmm. I taste raspberry yogurt, a warm snaking tongue around my own, and a tightening embrace so unimaginably delightful that I forget everything, where I am, or who I am.

My first kiss.

A bell dings with the rising of each floor. We kiss through the first floor... our faces squish together, twisting and turning...

Second floor... my tongue is getting fatigued...

Third floor—ding.

Emilee leaps away from me in an instant and grabs my hand in hers while we wait for the doors to open. Shoot, I wish Unit 13 was on the thirteenth floor. We step out and begin our walk down the winding maze of corridors to Unit 13. We don't speak. We smile a lot. I want to elope with Emilee. I want to father her children. This night feels like it's precariously balanced on a star light-years away from Earth, and I don't want it to fall off.

"There they are," says Ariel, looking up from her charting. "How'd it go, you two?"

"Greeeeeat," I say in almost a stupor. Emilee gives my hand a final squeeze and a mischievous wink and walks back to her room. I clumsily bump into the front desk, still a bit woozy from my ride with Emilee.

"Whoa there, soldier," says Ariel.

"Yeah," I say dreamily, resting my arm on the counter. I speak the truth before my thoughts have a chance to rework anything in my brain. "You know, Ariel, this night is definitely an experience I need to record in my journal. So much has happened, so many good things—and not just tonight..."

Ariel sets down her pen, leans back in her chair with a squeak, and folds her arms, listening.

"This entire hospital experience from day one has knocked me around. I can't deny that it hasn't been a bed of roses every day, but you know as well as I do that I love this place. It's become like a drug to me, one I'm not sure I can ever quit cold turkey. But something happened with me tonight, something unlike anything up to this point in my treatment. For the first time in my life, I actually liked myself. Me."

Ariel smiles and nods her head, as if trying to humor me.

"No, really, for once I wasn't the guy who masquerades as me; I was the real me. It felt strange and awkward at times, but I was me. And I believe this new me can grow if I give it a chance."

My many weeks on Unit 13 seem to finally be paying off. I'm taking risks that I never thought I'd ever take in a million years. I'm finally sharing some genuine emotion with staff. Journaling is helping me release and make sense of the inner turmoil between what I want to do and what I think others want me to be. My stomach, though still feeling like I have a child's rubber floaty ring under my skin, is beginning to handle more calories to the point where I don't freak out as much when I eat. My eating disorder isn't as threatening as it used to be. And, best of all, I received my very first date with a girl tonight, topped off with the most magnificent kiss I've ever had in my life. Of course, it's the only kiss I've ever had in my life, other than pecks on the cheek from Mom when I was a little kid.

Ariel's mouth stretches out into wide clown smile. "She kissed you, didn't she?"

"Huh? No—well, yes—but...I guess what I'm trying to say is that I think I'm ready to go home—to stay."

"Really?" she says, trying to disguise a snicker. "Wow, in that case, she must have really planted a wet one on you."

"Ariel! What kind of a thing is that to say?"

"I'm sorry, Gary. That was a little insensitive, I know. But keep in mind one night of wonderment does not make a lifetime. Your emotions are in somewhat of a haze right now, and I'd hate for you to be disappointed when the fog starts to burn off."

"But I believe I really am ready to go home, and it's not just because Emilee kissed m—"

Ariel lifts her chin and lowers her eyes. "I thought so."

"Well..." I admit, turning red, "I'm feeling confident that it's time to end this drudgery of an eating disorder campaign. My journaling is helping me to put life into perspective. I'm learning I want to do more with my life than exercising, counting calories, and being a slave to my routines and rituals. I'm missing out on so much. I'm sick of being sick."

"I'm very happy you feel that way, Gary, and I applaud your resolve to bow to a new outlook. It's just that, well, I'm afraid you're operating on high-octane emotions right now—both of you are. And when they go away, what will become of your newfound attitude?"

"Still the same, really."

You're thinking wrong.

No, you're not. You're simply going through change.

"It's important for you to understand that recovery is going to be a progressive process. Old messages die hard. Although I admit, a turnaround must be started somewhere."

See, you don't know what the heck you're doing.

Yes, you do. Swallow your pride. Listen to her.

"How are you feeling?" says Ariel. "And be honest."

I sigh. "Excited, but also let down, mainly because it's humbling to learn new things."

"I didn't mean to burst your bubble, Gary, and I don't deny that you have made a decision to turn a new leaf," Ariel says. "Just please keep in mind that staff observations are not meant to make you feel good. Change will not always be this comfortable, but it will get you another step closer to giving this beast a proper burial."

Ariel is right. She's absolutely right. I trust her, and I'm going to prove to her and myself that I don't need my eating disorder anymore.

"I'm going to do some journaling now," I say, stretching and yawning.

"Thanks for the talk, Ariel."

"No problem, Gary. What do we say I recommend to Dr. Buckmier and Greta a final discharge pass next week?"

"You're on."

CHAPTER THIRTY-EIGHT

BAD NEWS

Sure enough, a week later I stand on the scale in the examination room, waiting for it to register my weight. I'm as eager as a child waiting for his parents to give him the okay to rip open his birthday present. C'mon...c'mon...

"Stand still, Gary," gripes Atalanta. "I can't get an accurate reading."

"Sorry."

"110 pounds. Okay, you're done. How'd your night go last night with Emilee?"

"Oh, uh, good, thanks."

Now get out. I'm in a hurry. I need to get dressed, meet with Dr. Buckmier, grab some chow in the cafeteria, and get back up here before Emilee leaves on her pass for the weekend.

"Well, I'm glad you enjoyed yourself, but you're going to have to keep your jets cooled with her while on the unit. She has her own issues to work out too, you know, and you don't want to be distracting each other.

"We won't."

Jeez, Atalanta, did the guy stand you up on prom night, or did he use you to get to your best friend?

Dr. Buckmier says my weight is still way below normal limits for someone my age and size, but at a livable stage—out of the danger zone. Discharge is scheduled for Monday.

"It's a lovely day out there today," says Dr. Buckmier, opening my chart in the sunroom. "We have bright sunshine and no clouds. How're you doing?"

Prove yourself. You are capable.

"I'm doing fine," I say with optimism. A key is inserted into my back, and I'm instantly altered into a talking wind-up. "I'm looking forward to discharge on Monday. I can't wait to go home. I had a super evening last week with Emilee and some pretty good therapy sessions over the last week, in more ways than one. Journaling has been really enlightening for me. There's this YOU voice, you see, and it squares off with my eating disorder, and..."

For the next twenty minutes, I give the play by play of every significant transformational moment I've had since I was readmitted. Dr. Buckmier writes zealously in my chart. After a while, he gently sets his golden pen on his lap and just looks at me. There's a mystifying renovation taking place right in front of his eyes. For the first time I can remember, I feel confident in my ability to create constructive change in my life—and be okay with it. I have much of my journey ahead, but for now, I'm happy being in this present state. It feels so good to be okay with me—imperfect, but still under construction.

"That's wonderful, Gary," says Dr. Buckmier, decked out in a large, satisfied grin. "It sounds like a good time to start you on your final pass before we give you the final boot. How does this weekend sound?"

"Sounds like a plan."

"We'll see if you can maintain your weight. If you don't lose pounds, and your family session goes well Sunday night, we'll think about discharge early next week."

A small jolt rattles my spine. "Family session?"

"It's nothing major. It provides for an opportunity for closure and reflection with all involved. Eating disorders stem from intricate family issues. It's not some illness you concocted in isolation. A family session can work out any kinks that might impede your transition back to normal life at home."

I scurry to my room after the session to grab my cafeteria ID. Dr. Buckmier went longer than anticipated, putting me way behind schedule, so that means I have to fly through breakfast in order to get back up here to say good-bye to Emilee for her—

Emilee walks quickly up the corridor, sobbing like a baby. She sees me and rushes to my arms, burrowing her face into my shirt.

"What's up, Em?" I put my arms around her and pat her back.

Her hearty wailing prevents any form of understandable speech at first, but then she lifts her face from my chest, looking down. "Oh, Gary... I—I—I—"

"Take your time and relax. Speak slowly. What's wrong?"

"I-I-I'm be-be-be-being discharged this a-a-a-a-afternoon."

I feel as if a stone dropped into the pit of my stomach. "What? How come so soon?"

"They say I'm at a stage that can be managed through outpatient treatment. My parents will be coming to pick me up after lunch. Oh, Gary, I don't want to go home, not back there, with everything being the way...well, you know. I'll miss you."

"You mean, you haven't told anyone what's been happening?"

"Well, some of it, but not the... Well, not *those* parts."

Igor pushes the breakfast cart up the corridor. I pull Emilee into the group room away from the gathering patients and shut the door. I'm almost hysterical, but keep my voice down.

"Emilee," I say, looking serious, "you have to tell the staff what you told me. They can help you. You can't let your dad or that ogre ex-boyfriend of yours treat you like this anymore. You have to be strong."

Emilee's tears begin to rain on my arm once again. "I can't, Gary. You have a loving family. You have no idea how complicated this is. I just can't."

"Emilee," I respond firmly, squaring her up to my eyes, "listen to me. Unless you say something, you will continue to get abused. Remember last week, how wonderful it was for us? You deserve to have these loving feelings and a safe, happy life, just like I do. There are caring people out there who will help you and make sure you're safe. Trust me, Emilee. You have to trust me."

"Well, what about you? You've never told anyone about the bully. How can you tell me to—"

"You're right, Emilee," I say firmly, trying not to shout. "You're absolutely right. I know, it's very hard, not knowing what he'll do or— tell you what, maybe we could tell someone together. You know, I could support you."

"I don't know, Gary. It's still really scary." She looks away for a second, still panicked. "So what if we do tell and someone does help us. There's no telling what Mark will do to me when the heat has cleared."

"Well, I think we have to—"

She hugs me tightly again. Her hair smells fruity. After a minute of muted sobbing, she lifts her chin close to mine, looking deeply into my pupils, wanting to escape. Her lips draw closer to mine and—

"What's going on in here?" barks Atalanta, swooshing the door open, her wrinkled face contorted. "You two, get out here. Gary, you need to hike your little butt down to the cafeteria before they stop serving breakfast. Emilee, come with me."

My first thought is to skip breakfast and comfort Emilee, but I don't want to go rounds with Atalanta. Plus, I'm looking forward to waffles this morning, and I don't want to mess up my protocol right now since I'm so close to being discharged.

I race down the stairwell to the cafeteria, nearly knocking over a nurse carrying several large boxes of gauze bandages. I snatch a tray from the stack.

"Slow down there, Spike," says one of the Beefy Berthas. "What's the..."

"I'll take whatever."

"The waffles are a little—"

"Sounds great. Toss 'em on."

"Where's your sweethe—?"

"Upstairs, doing fine, thanks for the waffles, gotta go."

A nurse scans my ID card, but it doesn't take. "Dumb thing, I wonder what's the matter with it," says the attendant, popping the machine top off.

Oh, come on—not now!

After a minute of futzing with the machine, the attendant finally rings up my food. I rush to the first table I see and scarf down a waffle with syrup, Wheaties, and a glass of juice. Within five minutes I'm zinging back up the stairwell.

I frantically search for Emilee. She's nowhere in sight.

I check with Hadie. "She's not to be disturbed right now, Gary." *Sniff.* "She's with her nurse and needs to pack after that," *Sniff, sniff.* "Don't worry, you'll be able to see her after group therapy." *Sniff.*

I head to the group room and sit.

Group therapy is a sparse gathering this morning. Many patients are sick or out on passes. There's only five of us: Stanley the button man; two ancient, drugged-up depressed women in wheelchairs; and a fresh admittee named Irene. She's an eccentric middle-aged woman who apparently suffered a nervous breakdown in the middle of her keynote speaking engagement for the Advancement of Technological Garbage Disposals Convention and threatened to hotwire her newly patented garbage compactor into a bomb. She's wiry, straight-lipped, and bespectacled, and has graying, spiky, short hair. Emilee hasn't shown up yet.

Arty and Doreen are at their usual opposite sides of this morning's significantly reduced circle of chairs. Both sip fresh cups of coffee. Arty gets right down to business.

"So, Gary," he says, scratching his black beard, "I heard Monday is the big day."

I'm not intimidated any longer by his direct communication. "Yup, I can't wait. I didn't used to be able to say that, but I'm getting sick of this whole anorexia thing. I want out. It's time to move on with my life."

You're just doing another fanciful job at pleasing them again, aren't you?

No, you're not. You're being sincere.

"Yeah," I continue, "I wish I didn't even have to go on this pass this weekend and just simply go home today."

"Yeah, well, it's all part of the process," replies Arty, taking a sip of coffee "and it provides you an opportunity to prove yourself. Think of it as a self-confidence booster. Greta informed me that your family session will take place in this room on Sunday evening when you get back from your pass."

Irene blurts in. "Functioning at peak capacity within the disturbing dynamics of a nuclear family unit has the potential to compound inner intricacy patterns of behavior, thereby necessitating the user to display subconscious capabilities to dispel innate destructive drives."

The group just stares at her. How do you respond to that?

"A bomb, huh?" Arty states to Irene, turning the group's steering wheel. "How terrifying for you, Irene. How did you feel in the heat of the moment?"

"Well... I, uh... I guess I felt...like a subatomic undercurrent zipping through altered voltage transformers with only two electromagnetic frequencies."

"So you felt shocked and scared?" says Arty.

Irene looks astonished, with one hand pressed to her chest. "Isn't that what I just delineated?"

I really need to get out of here. Where's Emilee?

Ariel interrupts group. "Excuse me, Arty, but I need to steal Gary for a few moments."

Again?

We head to the dining room, where Emilee sits alone. I pull up a chair directly in front of her and take her hand into mine. Ariel shoos away a patient who wants to sneak another cup of coffee.

"I can't make you do anything you don't want to do, Emilee, but I'd wish you'd reconsider telling someone."

"I promise you, Gary, I'll think about it." She reaches down to her wrist and rips off her Unit 13 ID, plucks a strand of her silky black hair from the side of her head, and ties it around the bracelet. "Here, I'm not going to need this anymore, and I want something for you to remember our time together up here."

My heart cracks down the middle. "Thanks, Emilee, but we'll see each other soon. I'd give you mine, but I can't leave until Monday."

"Well, hey, at least you're doing much better. I'm so proud of you, Gary. You've come a long way. You're going to do great things someday. Just keep listening to your real self."

I give her an appreciative nod. We double check each other's notes to make sure our addresses and phone numbers are correct.

"This isn't really the end, you know," Emilee says. "We'll write and call, and maybe we can get together really soon."

"That sounds great."

Chattering adult voices materialize. Ariel appears around the corner talking with a gangly, professionally outfitted woman with a gleaming smile across her face. "Emilee, your mother's here."

"Hi, Em," says her mom, her eyes wavering to me. "Are you ready to get going home?"

She begins to move into the dining room when Ariel tugs her arm, cordially holding her back and whispering something into her ear. Emilee's mother nods her head approvingly. "We'll just wait up at the front desk, okay? But you're going to have to hurry things along. I only have a minute or so." They disappear up the corridor.

Emilee sighs very deeply. "Well, here I go. Wish me luck."

"What do you say about right now, Emilee? Just you and me, telling Ariel—"

"I don't know, Gary," says Emilee, eyes darting back and forth under pressure. "I appreciate your bravery to support me, but I'm not sure if I... I don't know."

She kisses me on the cheek, then grabs my hand and walks to the front desk.

"Ready, honey?" says Emilee's mom.

"Yes, Mom." She turns to me, holding both of my hands in hers, thinking, yearning to do the right thing. "Well...bye, Gary. I guess this is...Tell you what, I'll write to you as soon as I tell someone, okay?"

Emilee leaves quietly, looking back at me with grief. It's not exactly how I wanted it. I head to my room, flop backwards onto my bed, tuck my arms behind my head, and stare blankly at the dots on the ceiling tiles.

Ariel knocks on my door. "Are you okay, Gary?"

For the first time in my life, I ignore a nurse. It came naturally, so I go with it.

Ariel gets the hint. "I understand. I'll leave you be. If you need me, I'll be helping Stanley get out from under the pool table. He got stuck there while looking for a button. Oh, by the way, your mother called, and she's going to be picking you up in twenty minutes for your pass."

"I can't wait."

Liar.

CHAPTER THIRTY-NINE

MUSICAL TOAST

The next morning is Saturday, and it's business as usual at home. Dad has me help him shovel snow—two hours worth. We don't talk much because the work is strenuous. This used to be one of my favorite ways to burn calories, and if feels so exhilarating putting my muscles through a workout other than the non-aerobic exercise videos or casual strolls around the block, but it's lost its allure today because of my Emilee depression.

The urge to burn more calories comes crawling back into my psyche, but surprisingly, it's rather weak. YOU now commands the wheel. It seems I'm gradually turning into a different person. After shoveling, I choose to go and watch some TV instead of running around the block in snow boots. Grief over Emilee's departure has sapped the energy right out of me. In some way, I relish that I'm finally at the point where I'm able to actually say no to my incessant urge to exercise. But I'm also longing to retrieve those euphoric feelings of floating on cloud nine with

Emilee nestled within my arms. I've never felt this type of ache in my heart before. It feels harsh and hopeless with a sharp edge of permanence to it. I never thought I'd say this, but I'd rather feel the dreadful fattening sensation after meals than suffer through any more of this type of hurt.

Sunday morning brings church and brunch. My family is in the kitchen scampering about in their usual Sunday morning pattern. Dad mans the griddle: fried eggs, toast, bacon, doughnuts—a small buffet, the Grahl tradition for years on Sunday after church. It's the only day Mom allows Dad even near a cooking utensil. Why? I have no clue. No one asks. There's only one chore Dad leaves to the rest of us: toast patrol.

I usually volunteer for the fear of my mother involving herself in some underhanded scheme to slap some extra butter on my bread. I like my toast just right—not too crispy, not too floppy, with extra fat-free jelly and limited butter. Generally, I make everyone else's pieces first and pile them on a plate before I carefully construct my slice to utter perfection. One time, I went through an entire loaf of bread before I was finally satisfied. I kept chucking slices out the window for the birds when no one was looking or tucked them away in my pockets so my folks wouldn't put up a big stink.

Once it's fashioned to a primo delicacy, I place my piece of toast on the table before anything else gets set out. I never include my slice on the plate with the rest of the family's toast. This ensures that no one will mistakenly grab my slice amongst the lesser fatty pieces.

As I walk back to clean up my work area, Dad comes huffing and puffing by my shoulder, en route to the table. Horror kidnaps my placid emotions. He confiscates my perfectly constructed work of art and places it on the plate with the rest of the toast.

"You can leave that there," he says curtly, making his way back to the griddle to continue his flipping-of-the-sputtering-bacon ritual.

You must protect your world. You must duel.

Tell him how you feel.

"Dad, I'm upset that you did that," I say, asserting my new attitude. "This is my piece of toast. I don't want it mixed up with the rest."

Good job.

I gently pick up my slice, carefully scrape off all specks of non-diet jam, and gingerly deposit it onto the table by my place setting. Dad does an about face in a fury and throws it back on the plate with the rest of the toast.

"This will stay here, Gary," he shouts, saliva spraying everywhere. "You can eat it like the rest of us."

Great, now I have germs splattered all over my piece.

Stand your ground.

Wait, was that YOU or my eating disorder?

"No, I won't," I say angrily, snatching my toast and tenderly holding it in my hands.

Dad grits his teeth.

My lips purse shut.

His mouth contorts.

My blood boils.

His face grows red with rippling wobbles.

My toast squishes in my hand.

His white knuckles clasp the greasy spatula handle as he hoists it into the air.

"For heaven's sake, don't!" shouts Mom. "Take it easy!"

My mouth begins to open.

Do not go there. Get away in the other direction. It will be easier that way.

YOU? Where are you?

And then, the weirdest thing happens: I begin to laugh.

"Gary," says Mom. "What are you laughing at?" There's nothing funny about this."

You should be ashamed of yourself.

Wait a minute, not so fast. You said to get away in the other direc—

Oh, so now you're listening to me again? Good boy.

But I feel so—

Don't, okay? It will be too disturbing.

YOU? Where are you? Come on.

I make a dive for my room and slam the door. I'm such a stupid... How can I be so...? Why do I listen to...? Ariel was right. I'm slipping back and allowing my emotions to make my decisions. I'm such vermin.

You can say that again.

SHUT UP!

Calm down, Gary.

I don't give a—Where were you a minute ago?

I've always been here. You simply need to make the choice to—

There's your baseball bat. Grab it. Hammer the dresser. It will upset your folks, and you deserve their vengeance.

I reach for my autographed Jim Gantner baseball bat and slam it down on the dresser with a vengeance. The heavy piece of furniture is so solidly structured that my bat barely even dents the glossy surface. Serves me right—I can't even destroy something properly. I lift my bat for a second smash when Mom sweeps open the door.

Uh, oh—this is going to hurt.

I feel—

Don't.

But, I was just going to tell everyone—

Don't. You hear me? Do NOT!

"*Gaa*-ry! What do you think you're doing?" screeches Mom. "Put that bat down!"

My breathing is heavy. I feel lightheaded.

"You're going to be responsible for any damages, young man. I can't believe you're doing this again. Who are you?

Mutant. Freak.

My bat flings through the air, ricocheting off the wall and onto my bed.

"I can't stand this anymore. That's it! I'm calling Greta right now," says Mom, huffing hard with quaking hands. "And wipe that smirk off your face. This is serious."

She throws me The Look.

Duck.

My eating disorder brands me deep, throwing YOU up against the ropes. Mom pulls the door shut with such ferocity that the vibrations cause two baseball helmets from my collection to jitter from the shelf and clunk onto the floor.

You are such a manipulative little monster. How could you take advantage of your own mother like that?

Just calm down. You're going to be okay. Breathe. Refocus.

"Aaaaaaaah!"

My unrestrained hands snatch my bat from my bed and smash it down onto one of the many sports trophies decorating my dresser, decimating the hard plastic.

You're weakening.

I fling my bat across the room, puncturing a gaping hole into the drywall, and plunk down onto my bed in the fetal position. My sweaty hands hide my face beginning to moisten with tears—my breathing reminiscent of a raging bull. Forty-five minutes take hours.

You're not normal. You realize that, don't you?

I'm swept up, once again, in a vicious whirlwind of irrationality. IT just doesn't want to end. I hate IT. I hate IT. I hate IT.

You are worthless, insignificant, unimportant. You are a problem, a waste of time. Get your UPS package.

I duck under my bed and pull out an old shoe box.

It's going to be okay, Gary.

No, I'm not. I'm such a stupid idiot. I uncover the box and pull out—

You're capable, Gary. Remember what Ariel talked about. Old habits are hard to break. Change is gradual. You don't need to do this.

You thought you could do it, to change old habits, but you can't. You're useless.

No, you're not. Put the knife down, Gary.

No, I've been asking for this for a long time.

The genuine imitation *Rambo* survival knife is gripped tightly in my right hand. Its ten-inch, razor-sharp blade rests across my chest, and begins to embed under my nipple. Movie scenes of Johnny *Rambo*'s graphic torture fuel intense self-hatred. My wrist is next. Before I can think too much about what I'm doing, and before goose bumps are sliced away, there's a gentle knock at the door. I pitch my knife under the bed and hastily tuck my shirt into my pants before the door slowly cracks open to disclose Dad's face. "Come on, Gary. We're going back to the unit."

CHAPTER FORTY

THE SESSION

"Gary?" says Ariel, knocking on the heavily secured Quiet Room door. "May I come in?"

I'm one giant mass of prickly thistles. "Whatever."

Ha, ha, ha. What a piece of work.

Ariel walks in and leans on the wall next to a wobbly old cot, folding her arms.

"So," she says, "I understand you're having an extremely difficult time this morning. What seems to be the problem?"

I say nothing. I care about nothing. I just want to be left alone.

"Why don't you just say 'I told you so' and get it over with?" I say in a depressed tone.

Ariel ignores my comment, and says, "You understand that you will not be discharged unless you go through the family session." She's apparently not intimidated by my bitter gall.

"But I screwed up and had a horrible pass."

"Well, yes and no," says Ariel. "Yes, you chose to vent your anger in a violent manner, but then again, you did show your anger. I see it as progress. Change does not happen overnight, you know. Your brother and parents are here now, so we might as well get the show on the—"

"Can't you see I don't give a crap about them? I know, it's a selfish thing to say. I don't even know how or why I'm saying such terrible words, but welcome to my life!"

Pitiful, just pitiful.

I can't believe what just flew out of my mouth. I must have freaked Ariel out. She begins to grin, which turns to a chuckle shortly thereafter.

"Good for you," says Ariel, smiling and shaking her head. "The staff has been waiting a long time to be introduced to this side of you. Pity they aren't here to enjoy the scene."

What a putrid hunk of vile—

You didn't break her. Your anger is okay. She's okay. You're okay.

My bubbling volcanic anger smolders and cools.

How did she do that?

"The way I see it," she says, "you can continue giving your eating disorder ammunition to fire at you, or you can chalk this up as another learning experience to feed your new self."

I give no response—only sighs, one of my trademarks now. Of course, she calmed me down in seconds, something no one has ever done—

Don't listen to her. She's another one trying to control you.

You think so?

You're capable of doing this.

"How are you doing right now, Gary?" asks Ariel. "You seem preoccupied. Talk to me."

My fingers clutch my face. "I don't know what to say, except that I'm sorry for yelling at you like that."

"No need to apologize for having feelings," says Ariel. "If that were the case, we'd all be spending most of our days saying we're sorry to everyone—although we'll have to work on your approach."

You really are capable, Gary. One mistake does not make you a failure. Never has, never will.

A pinch of confidence surfaces once again and begins tickling at my awareness.

"You got yourself a job to do right now," Ariel says, "one that's important for you and the rest of your family. I suggest you get on out there and give it your best shot. It ain't gonna hurt 'em."

"I don't know, Ariel."

"You don't know what?"

You are worth the effort.

"Well..." I say, fearful of the next words coming forth from my lips, "I'm afraid of...of..."

Don't you dare, it will—

"Just say it," says Ariel. "I can take it."

You're perfectly capable. Go on. Feelings are normal.

"Okay, okay... I'm afraid of feelings, of what I might say, of how they'll react, of the looks on their faces..."

"Hey, look at that," says Ariel, holding up her hand for a high five, which I oblige with hesitation. "You're two for two. Good work. Now, let's get out there and make it three for three, okay?"

You can do it. You'll be just fine.

No you—

Concentrate on what you need to do. Acknowledging your feelings will keep your eating disorder in check. Don't allow it to captain the ship.

I take a deep breath and let it out slow and strong. "I don't know. I'm getting so sick and tired of getting whipped around like a boat in a storm. First I'm up, feeling confident and great, then the next day I'm drowning. There's no consistency to it all. It seems I end up going to such extremes, too. How long is this going to last?"

"Quite a while, to be honest, but you learn to pocket what you've learned along the way, which builds up your nerve to make change happen. Recovery and change is ongoing, a process... Process, process,

process—not an end in itself."

I sigh, letting out a smattering of frustration.

"Come, let's get going, okay? I trust you're going to handle this just fine."

Ariel escorts me out of the Quiet Room by the hand. Mom and Dad are already seated on a noisy leather couch next to Rick. They all laugh and act as if they're at a party waiting for the guest of honor to arrive. I sit in a chair opposite Ariel.

"Well, Grahl family," Ariel begins, taking a deep breath, "thank you for coming. This is not easy for anyone involved, but Greta thought this best after taking your phone call, Mom."

Bright smiles get pitched all around. We are highly-trained professionals at masking genuine emotion—at the moment, embarrassment and nervous curiosity. Ariel begins with the ground rules. She's direct, to the point, and stays objective. Arty has clearly taught her well. This is followed by a series of reflective questions about the events of the morning.

For the first few minutes, all we do is display our dental work in silence, each hoping the other takes the lead. We are great followers, like wandering baby geese hoping to find our mother on a busy freeway. And then...

"I just don't understand why Gary doesn't want to eat," says Rick. "He does so well in sports... I would think he'd want to eat to get back in action."

Ariel points to me while looking at Rick, and says, "He's sitting over there. Why don't you ask him?"

This is going to be excruciatingly difficult. Stick to what has worked in the past: people pleasing.

"How come you don't eat?" he asks with a pout.

Stay silent.

That won't do you any good. Just be honest with him, just like you did with Ariel a moment ago. He won't break.

"I'm afraid of...of...well, getting fat," I say, taking a quick peek into his eyes, and then back to the legs of his chair. "I know it sounds weird, but it's the truth."

You see, it wasn't as gut wrenching as you thought. Remember,

you've been down this road before, and you survived just fine.

"But you're not fat," says Rick, looking extremely uneasy. "Can't you see that?"

Don't answer. Just smile. It will only get worse for you.

"*Gaa*-ry," says Mom.

See, I told you. It's going to be uncomfortable.

So what if it's uncomfortable. You can handle it.

"We just want what's best for you," says Mom. "We...we...."

"You what, Mrs. Grahl?" asks Ariel.

"Well..." Mom continues, obviously struggling to spit out the words that are hitting her right in the face, "...you know...we love you, Gary."

Eeewwwwww! Why do we need to do this?

It's simply a feeling. Feelings are—

—not okay. Remember that, you filthy wretch. Feelings are not okay.

Once again, the room is swallowed up by a hushed stillness. We'd rather be getting a series of rabies shots in the stomach. Mom sighs. Dad is somber and has that I-think-I'm-going-to-cry look. My brother does a lot of shifting in his chair. This is obviously extremely uncomfortable for him—and the rest of us, to be honest.

"Well, it looks like we might be here a while," says Ariel, not allowing us off the hook. "What's happening right now?"

We all fit on our smile masks again. My breathing begins to swell from resentment. I'm sick and tired of being locked up in this little prison. I want freedom to be me—whoever that is. I experienced it just yesterday.

Tell them how you feel. It's okay.

This is an outrage. How can you stand for this? Remain quiet.

I sigh—twice.

"I don't understand how he can't see that we're trying to help him," Dad says to Ariel. "If he knows food will make him healthy and strong to play ball, why doesn't he do it?"

"He's over there, remember?" Ariel points at me.

"Don't you see we're trying to help you, Gary?" Dad's eyes droop, his voice stammering.

Remain silent.

You know you want to tell him. Go ahead. You'll be fine.

I stare fixedly at his chair legs, and then say, "Yeah, I know. I know you're trying to help me. That's the problem. You're all being so nice and supportive, and I'm spitting it right back in your face."

You insensitive jerk.

"How do you feel about what Gary said, Mr. Grahl?" Ariel asks.

"I understand that he thinks that way, but—"

"Yes," Ariel interjects, "but how do you feel?"

This is too touchy feely. Don't look at him.

"How do I feel?" asks Dad, evidently stalling for time. We all do it so effortlessly. "I guess I feel...sort of frustrated. Yeah, I feel frustrated."

Ariel looks back to me, smiling, with one eyebrow hoisted to her bangs.

I mutter, "I guess I feel..." and then drag out another long grave sigh.

No. Don't do it.

Feelings are okay. Do it.

"I feel so...embarrassed right now for even being here. I've come to believe that feelings and talking are not okay in this family, and I'm upset..."

What are you doing? Are you nuts?

Keep going. You're doing the right thing.

"... I'm upset with...with you, Mom and Dad, for not—"

"*Gaa*-ry!" cries Mom, giving me The Look. "How can you say that? You know perfectly well you can talk to us about anything."

Yeah, and that's why you won't let me finish my sentence, right?

How can you be so callous with your folks?

I feel totally out of line. The tension in the room is so thick that it could be sliced with a knife. It's as if I don't know my own parents—strangers with whom I've had little emotional connection over the years. I feel awkwardly guilty for it.

You have done nothing wrong. You are simply not used to showing feelings, that's all. Expressing genuine emotion in a

respectful way over time will change that. That's what being you is all about.

Are you sure I'm doing the right thing?

Yes. It will feel uncomfortable, but it's healthy. The road to health is not always the one that feels good.

You are an outcast. You don't deserve to live. You don't deserve to have this loving family of yours.

"How do you feel, Mrs. Grahl, about what Gary said?" Ariel asks.

"I just can't believe how you can feel that way, Gary. You know you're—"

"I'm sorry, Mrs. Grahl," Ariel interrupts once again, "but I want you to focus on your own feelings, not Gary's feelings. He's capable of handling his own."

Mom sighs, slowly and steadily—it runs in the family. She hates hearing this probably more than I hate doing it.

"W-well," she stammers, "I feel upset that he thinks—"

Ariel butts in with frustration. "Maybe we better outfit Gary in blaze orange camouflage so you can all see him. Folks, it's important to speak to the person you're addressing."

"Sorry," says Mom, giving a quick laugh, which gives way to a huge smile. "I feel upset that you would think that way."

See, you upset her.

No, you didn't. Say what you want to say. You're doing fine.

The urge to let go—to burst free—swells through me like an ocean squall.

"Like right now," I say, actually looking into my mother's flustered eyes. "I don't understand how come you're smiling when we are obviously upset. It's like there's an elephant in the room that we're all pretending is not there, and I feel..."

Don't!

Take your control back.

"I feel wrong," I say, the red in my face slowly turning back to my normal color. "I feel cheated and manipulated. I feel angrier than all get out! I don't want to feel these feelings because I feel guilty, scared, and wrong. I can't do this anymore! I don't want to do this anymore..."

What am I doing? I can't believe I'm say these things.

That's it. Embrace the relief. You'll be fine. So will your family. Give them a little credit. They can take it.

I keep going. "I'm sick of having this stupid eating disorder. I don't want to be angry with you, although I can't help but harbor a...well...it's, like...this uncleanness so deep inside me that I can't reach down and get a hold of it to do anything about it. I'm sorry I had to drag you all through this garbage, but I need help. I have a problem..."

You are the problem!

The problem is not you. The struggle is the eating disorder. These are two separate things. The time has now come to stop obeying IT. Keep going.

"I have been nothing but an arrogant, selfish, royal liar to all of you. I'm sorry. I'll do whatever I need to do to get rid of this thing. Thank you for being there for me. You are such a wonderful family. I love you all very much."

I feel the weight of the world dropping off of my shoulders with a monstrous thump.

"Well, we love you, too, Gary," says Dad with tears streaming down his cheeks.

A thin black smear begins trickling from Mom's left eye—eyeliner—as she fights off tears of her own. She says, "Of course we love you, Gary. You're our son, and we will always be here for you. We would do anything for you."

Say what you're thinking—respectfully, of course.

"Speaking of which, I feel resentful at times when you guys do too much for me. I understand you're just trying to show your love and concern and want to help, but I want to do things for myself now."

What are you doing? This is utterly—

Shut up, IT. Don't interrupt.

"Like that time, Dad, when you pulled my mitt out of my hands to help me restring it. I wanted to do the lacing myself."

My hands start quivering as I find my mouth shooting off with reckless abandon. I grunt through the urge to look back at my eating disorder for directions. Instead, I choose to listen to the throbbing ache in my body—that of chained emotion screaming for freedom.

"And then there are the double messages... Mom, when you told me I might get fat after my third helping of ice cream after the many times you've gone off about me having the genes to eat anything I wanted... Well, that doesn't make sense to me." Now that I've gotten started, it's getting easier and easier. "I wanted to say something, but I didn't want to deal with a conflict, mainly because it doesn't seem okay in our family. I want us to be able to talk openly with each other about these sensitive issues without the fear of being rejected."

With each passing word, with every feeling I resolutely cut from bondage, I breathe in fresh, healing air. Although it feels alien, it's invigorating nonetheless. My family is proving without a shadow of a doubt that they're capable of handling these foreign words from my lips and touchy-feely emotions from my heart that I thought would mortify them.

You're giving them credit for being able to take care of themselves.

Ariel says nothing, but sits back, grinning and taking it all in. If I'm not mistaken, I swear she's proud of me—I know I am. My family sits eerily still with their mouths partway open. Shock needs time to wear itself down, but I'm confident they'll be just fine.

It feels great inside, knowing I'm heading in the right direction despite the stinging open sores of vulnerability. The cell door to my prison has been open for a long time. I push myself off the cold, damp floor once again, dust off my clothes, and stick my nose out to catch a whiff of freedom. Healing smells fresher this time around, and so worth the effort.

"Gary," says Ariel, "I must admit that I'm quite impressed. It's wonderful to see the real you. That shell of yours must get awful musty. How are you feeling right now?"

"Good. It feels so good to actually get this stuff off of my chest."

"I believe you're finally growing up," says Ariel, "in more ways than one."

My family's heads all nod in agreement.

"Gary, we want you to feel comfortable talking to us about whatever you want," says Dad. He sounds like he might start crying. "I'm proud of you for telling us how you feel. It's not going to hurt us." He lets off a slight chuckle, as if trying to bypass the tears that are still welling up in his eyes.

"Yes, you did a good job, Gary," says Mom. "We've been waiting a long time for you to get to this point."

Rick slouches in his chair. "You got that right," he agrees.

It feels—

Feel, feel, feel—is that all you can talk about?

At the moment, yes, so buzz off to where you ever came from. I'm so sick and tired of you—so indescribably sick and tired—that I never want to listen to you again.

Oh, but you will. You always end up crawling back to me after one of your little "highs." It's like clockwork with you.

You don't need to listen to your eating disorder anymore. You have a newer, more satisfying lifestyle beckoning for your attention.

Entertaining this whole internal battle with genuine emotions and thoughts is nothing short of exhausting, but not the horrid, blood and guts, painstaking struggle I thought is would be. I'm discovering I can do it, and survive. It's actually invigorating, especially when resting in the knowledge that I'm being me, and that's okay. I am a separate person, special in my gifts, talents, and personality. I am learning, making mistakes, and growing from them. Mistakes are okay.

I am not a mistake.

CHAPTER FORTY-ONE

COURAGE

Cough, cough. My eyes startle open as I sit in My Chair. Greta stands directly over me wearing a hearty smile.

"Pardon me if I scared you, Gary," she says. "Deep in thought, or shall I say, deep in prayer possibly?"

"Yeah," I say.

"I'd like to steal a few moments of your time if you don't mind."

"I think I can fit you into my busy schedule this evening," I reply, taking an open shot at comedy for a change.

Greta gives me a snort. "Follow me, please." She escorts me to her office, just off the smoking room. It's huge. The room reeks of old library—a smell I love for some reason. Row upon row of books cover three of the four off-tan walls that reach to a cathedral ceiling painted in chubby angelic beings. A small forest of plants and exotic trees that I only see in *National Geographic* sit in large pots surrounding various statue heads, tribal relics, and a variety of spinning objects that are generally purchased from one of those expensive junk catalogs my mom gets by the dozens in the mail.

Greta's desk is a colossal, half-moon, heavy oak design that probably took ten men to carry in here. Symmetrically placed around a sizeable bay window—now showing a sky turning dusk—are numerous diplomas, awards, and framed pictures of Greta engaged in extreme activities—mountain climbing, surfing, skydiving, and scuba diving.

"This one is my favorite," says Greta, handing me a small framed picture displaying her shaking hands with the President of the United States in the oval office. "It was a distinct honor I had last year to accompany a group of mental health professionals at a dinner gala at the White House."

My eyes continue inventory down Greta's wall where—

Aaah!

"Hello, Gary," says Ms. Wheeler. "How are you doing?"

My hand covers my chest with open fingers. "You scared the crap out me," I exclaim.

"Sorry about that," says Ms. Wheeler, "but I don't believe you have an ounce of crap in your entire body."

Greta cuts in. "Gary, won't you have a seat?" She extends her hand to a chair next to Ms. Wheeler. "Ms. Wheeler has something she wishes to tell you, and it might not meet with your dearest approval."

Huh?

"Well, Gary," sighs Ms. Wheeler, "I'll get right to the point. Mr. Rueter, myself, and some of your other teachers had a meeting this morning concerning your status. You've been doing a great job considering the circumstances...but..." She glances at Greta, who sits behind her desk with fingertips touching together in front of her face. "Mr. Rueter has noticed that you've really struggled with homework, and you've missed considerable classroom instruction. Let's just say that this just puts your chances of receiving any sort of quality education at a great disadvantage. Anyhow, what I'm trying to say is that we've, uh, we've decided that it would be in your best interests if you postponed academics for now and retook course work next year."

Immediately upon hearing the words "postpone academics," I feel immense relief.

Greta and Ms. Wheeler are silent, awaiting my reaction.

"You mean take my senior year over?"

"Well, not the entire year, just the classes you'll be missing," explains Ms. Wheeler. She tries to be sympathetic. "Look at it this way, you won't have to stress yourself out with homework, so you'll be able to concentrate on improving your health. Plus, you'll also be invited to two graduation reunions every five years."

I feel myself grinning.

"Gauging from your reaction, then," says Ms. Wheeler, "I take it that this news comes as a load off your mind?"

"Well, actually... yeah. Now I don't have to worry about school."

"I'm glad to hear that," says Ms. Wheeler, breathing a sigh of relief. "I was concerned that once you found out you won't be able to graduate with your class this year, you'd be extremely disappointed. This will also free up more mental energy to devote to your recovery."

"Yeah," I say, suddenly struck with a bit less enthusiasm. Her words sounded better at the beginning of her speech.

"And as soon as you're discharged, make an appointment with me to go over details. We'll discuss graduation and career plans at that time..."

Career plans? You mean molding depth finders at P.J. Puck isn't a valid profession?

"For now," says Ms. Wheeler, just concentrate on getting healthy."

I'm left in silence to ruminate on what just happened.

"Is there anything the matter, Gary?" asks Ms. Wheeler.

"Well... no."

Greta coughs, as if trying to send me a smoke signal. I can't read smoke language.

"Very well, then," says Ms. Wheeler. "I guess my job is done here for today."

"Thanks for coming in, Lucille," says Greta, getting up from her chair. "Allow me..." She escorts Ms. Wheeler to the door and quietly clicks it closed, then makes her way back behind her desk, carefully examining my body language the entire time. "You don't look like one happy to be departing the confines of a psychiatric unit, my boy. I take it all is not well?"

"No," I say with a sigh. "I'm excited—really I am. It's just that...well, I'm happy but I'm not happy, you know?"

I look at Greta, waiting for her to make some wise commentary, but she stays reserved.

"I know I've made improvements and all, but somehow, after I heard this news about me retaking my senior year over, I...it's just that, well, IT is still there."

"IT?" Greta asks, raising her brow. "Who do you think IT is?"

"Well, I understand IT is my anorexia, but I can't get the notion out of my mind that IT might be something much bigger that anorexia. In a creepy dream I had, IT bombarded my every decision. IT just won't go away, but then there's this YOU voice on the brain, the one that feeds me affirming commentary. It showed up shortly after my big crying episode last hospitalization. YOU fights IT—"

Greta quickly puts up her hand.

"Take it easy," she says, "slow down, although it's refreshing to see you exhibiting such exuberant authentic concern." She breathes a sigh of her own. "I believe, Mr. Grahl, we need to continue this conversation over a game of Scrabble. We've been blessed with a beautiful, winter evening. Let's go out onto the courtyard veranda, shall we? They've just installed the heated enclosures."

Now?

We make our way onto a gazebo in the center of the Saint Abernathy Hospital grounds. The falling sun creates a magnificent array of color over the horizon with a slight, crisp breeze gently shuffling the air—in short, it's a gorgeous evening.

I set up the board as I have done dozens of times during my stay. Greta and I play long after the staff ignite the boardwalk torches. For a while, our conversation stays light, but gradually it diverges to a more serious track. The board is just about full.

"What I don't understand is how long IT will stay in my head," I say, changing the subject from fifteen minutes of baseball banter.

"Many questions in this life are, unfortunately, left unanswered," says Greta. "This, I believe, might be one of them. And may I add, Gary, I think it's time to stop referring to your eating disorder as IT. There is absolutely no use in granting this illness any more power and attention than it deserves. Let me ask you: What if your eating disorder doesn't disappear? What then?"

"I don't know. All I want is to be happy, to feel free of this ball and chain," I position my last few letters on the board to form the word "foam."

"Freedom in your case is not a means to an end," says Greta, leaning forward on folded arms. "Freedom cannot be obtained after following a formula. No, true freedom is a state of mind, an attitude from within your heart that says 'I don't have control over everything and that's okay.' It's giving in to influences much greater than our petty problems. In other words, Gary, *letting go*." Greta pauses, and then fumbles with her remaining letters. "I believe it's my turn?"

"Oh, uh, yeah," I say, pondering everything she's telling me, "it's your turn."

Greta places down two letters that spell the word "out" which ends the game. I add up points. She then muses one final move for a few moments before her mouth curls into a wide grin, as if suddenly being enlightened. At first she does nothing, but then, without aborting her attentive gaze, she takes some letters from off the board and puts together one final word..

"Well," I say, "it looks as if age comes before beauty in Scrabble, too. You win."

"Yes, your eating disorder will, if you allow it," Greta says candidly, her grin still fixed on me.

"What do you mean?"

"Look." She motions with her eyes for me to look down at the table.

"S-H-A-M-E... shame," I say bewildered. It gradually leads to illumination. "So, you're saying that my villain—my IT voice—is shame?

Greta nods slightly.

I keep my stare fixed on the word, studying it like a last-minute test question I need to answer.

Greta explains, "Your eating disorder is only one aspect of what you called IT. Shame is a devastating thing, Gary. It buries its poison deep into the confines of our thinking, leaving its host feeling utterly helpless and worthless. But listen to me, Gary." She leans forward on her arms once again, attempting to reinforce the importance of her next words. "Shame can only be as strong as we allow it to be. Shame is not a feeling; it's more like a state of mind. Shame will not tell us that we have done something wrong; shame will tell us that *we* are wrong, defective, incapable and undeserving of anything good."

Hope percolates into my life with every word Greta utters.

"But I find myself feeding shame constantly," I say, "like I'm out of control and under extreme pressure to be a certain somebody that others will like, and can't do anything about it."

"Someone once said that the pressure to live up to fine potential is the greatest burden one can bear. But only if one believes God-blessed talent to be a hindrance. Ultimately, you are the one in charge of navigating your life course."

I shake my head in disgust. "Shame seems like a vicious Ferris wheel— shame, YOU, shame, YOU, shame, YOU. It doesn't make sense. When will it end?"

"Unfortunately," Greta continues, "that is a question that can only be answered by the one who poses it. Mental illnesses are not logical, and they don't make sense. Shame is a reality that does not go away easily with any fly-by-night formula, and can initiate great destruction—at times to a fatal end. Unless...now listen to me carefully, Gary, unless, of course, you attack its weakness and harness the secret."

"Weakness?"

"Mocking... shame hates to be mocked. The secret is to harness shame's destructive energy and direct it to more constructive means."

My mind races like it has never done before.

"Constructive means?"

"Yes," says Greta, "the ability to transform shame's caustic patterns into constructive, advantageous ends. For instance, have you ever stopped to think about how Jim Gantner pulls himself out of a hitting slump?"

"You know, he talked about that when he visited me. It had something to do with reshaping his thoughts onto reality at hand, like reminding himself of the fact that in order to get to the big leagues he needed to have an elite level of talent—and hard work."

"Most definitely... most definitely, indeed," says Greta, nodding in agreement, "just as you have been blessed with your own versions of talent."

"Me?"

"Oh yes, Gary. In fact, I'm surprised you haven't made this discovery yourself through your journaling exploits. I believe that in time you will."

"What are you talking about?"

"Have you any idea how much energy it takes to maintain an eating disorder?"

I pause for a moment. "Well...yes, I do."

"Talent number one," says Greta, pointing her index finger into the air, "self-determination. Not everyone possesses your level of drive and self-discipline, Gary. Do you have any idea how stubborn individuals with eating disorders are?"

I contemplate once more. "I'm not stubborn."

"See what I mean? Talent number two," says Greta, raising two fingers. "For some people, Gary, stubbornness can be a debilitating thorn in their side. Their visions to a successful future get so fogged up with pride that they lose direction. But learning to funnel stubbornness in constructive ways can be advantageous. The greatest influences for humanity over the generations owned the most stubborn minds. Positive change is hard. It mandates a certain level of unadulterated bullheadedness to achieve desired outcomes. I believe you have this."

Greta rests quietly for a moment and stares into my eyes, carefully evaluating the myriad thoughts bustling around in my head. "Do you know how sensitive many people with eating disorders are?"

"What do you mean by that?"

"The common stresses of life are difficult to cope with, most certainly, but to many people with eating disorders, stress is downright unbearable. They hold a temperament that is hyperaware of incoming stimuli and emotional hurt in their surroundings. What are considered little molehills of stress for some people can be construed as giant mountains for those with sensitive personalities." She pokes my arm and gives me a wink. "These types of people are IT's favorite targets because shame can easily manipulate their confidences. However, sensitive personalities are so specialized in their 'radar' capacities that they pick up details that others would never see in a million years. These people gravitate into the helping professions like social work, counseling, health care and end up saving lives in more ways than one. This, I believe, is talent number three for you. Need I go on?"

"I get the picture."

Greta seems to read me like her favorite book. I absolutely love how she can turn a negative perspective on its head and change it to a compliment. She is so incredibly wise and convinced, despite the fact she knows how harshly the years can erode a person's life. Her sheer, unabashed assurance is something I can only hope I'll achieve one day. I believe I am closer.

"But how do I start this process?" I'm eager to drink in more of Greta's advice.

"You've already begun," says Greta, cleaning up the Scrabble board. "Admitting your struggle publicly devalues shame and energizes YOU, reducing shame's power. Yet, shame won't go away without a vicious fight. Over time, Gary, the more you gravitate toward that optimistic YOU voice, as you call it, the harder and longer shame will fall—and remain down."

Greta has this way about her that makes me want to stand up and shout "I can do it!" I feel like I'm sitting in the locker room at school listening to my coach give the team a pep talk before going out onto the field for the second half of the game.

"I strongly recommend you continue developing your liking for journaling," Greta says. "Search out with words who you are—what you like, don't like, any genuine needs and wants. What do you believe in? What are your passions, activities that—barring all of the inhibiting powers of shame—you would truly enjoy doing? And most importantly, be open to sharing this new you with those you care about. Are you with me?"

Yeah! C'mon team, let's go out and kick some butt!

"You bet," I say. My sigh is deep, but I'm feeling optimistic.

"And one last thing, Gary," says Greta, digging for something in her sweater pocket. "It's helpful to begin setting your sights on things outside of yourself, like offering yourself to others. You will find the rewards are unmatched."

She pulls out two, large, individually wrapped chocolate chip cookies. She slides one across the table to me. "Here, I have an extra. Enjoy."

"Thanks," I say happily, secluding it inside one of my military pants pockets. "I'll have it later."

"Suit yourself," says Greta, putting the Scrabble game under her arm and getting up to leave. "Well, Gary, I need to be moseying back to the unit. Feel free to sit a spell if you'd like. I'll see you in the morning for discharge."

I never thought I'd say this, but I'm finally excited about returning home—my real home.

Chapter Forty-Two

Trash It

Dr. Buckmier must be writing a book. He's taking an awful lot of notes this morning.

"I understand congratulations are in order on two fronts," he says, banging his pen on the arm of the chair to wake up the ink. "You're up another pound this morning, and it sounds like you've won a much bigger battle internally."

I nod my head.

"Your weight is still a bit low according to my standards for discharge; however, it is progressing upward at a workable rate. More importantly, you've certainly shown evidence of working very hard to adjust the way you choose to cope with the extraordinary stresses of an eating disorder. And that, I believe, is deserving of another test run out in the field. Of course, I expect you to contact my office at your earliest convenience to set up a weekly outpatient schedule. You should be all set on amitriptyline for awhile, correct?"

I nod my head.

"Very well, then. I wish you the best of luck, my boy. You have chilly rain out there on departure. The old man has taken one on the chin."

"Hey, Doc, what do you mean by the old man?"

"Oh, that?" says Dr. Buckmier. "It's just my way of poking fun at the deep, inner influence." He pauses, as if searching for just the right word for the occasion. "Almost a voice, if you will, that drives us batty sometimes. I think it just gets in the way most of the time." He opens the sunroom door. "Well, shall we?"

"Before I go, Doc, do you have any final words of wisdom?"

Dr. Buckmier relaxes his grip on the doorknob, looking thoughtfully into the air. "Well, there is a quote I like to come back to every now and then: 'Remember where you've been, remember who you've met, remember how you've grown, remember who you are.'"

I grin. "I'll have to write that one down in my journal."

"Oh, and one last one," says Dr. Buckmier, our spindly hands locked in a firm shake. "This country has more than its share of talkers. It needs more listeners. I think you'd be excellent at that."

After one last cheery smile at each other, Dr. Buckmier welcomes his next patient, Floyd, who has been waiting by the door stretching some pantyhose back and forth like a kid playing with a rubber band. I chuckle and make my way up the corridor to the front desk.

"Take care, Gary," says Arty. "And did you notice I didn't warn your parents this time that you'll be back?"

We grip our hands in a rigid shake, almost like engaging in thumb wars to see who can squeeze the tightest, smiling confidently at each other. "I don't intend to be." I say. He surrenders his hold, pulling me in for a hug.

"Bye, y'all," says Wal-Mart. "Keep away from us, ya hear?"

"Will do," says Mom smiling, carrying a load of my clothes.

"You're a tough cookie," says Atalanta, smiling kindly at me for once. "Ever thought about the Marines as a career?

"Not this year," I say in jest, "but according to Greta," I glance at her standing behind the desk, "I have the stubbornness to manage."

Greta winks.

Ariel escorts Mom and me to the entrance, where Mom has pulled up the car so we don't have to fight the rain. "Well, take care, Gary. To say it's been a privilege to know you is an understatement. Oh, I almost forgot, here, take this..." She hands me a small wrapped gift. "This is a little something to get you to loosen up. I want to see the fruit of your labor sometime soon."

I tear into the wrapping paper like a boy on Christmas morning. "A juggling kit?"

"Yeah," says Ariel, snatching three bean bags from the box and juggling them effortlessly in the air. "I plan to see regular progress during outpatient weigh-ins, just like this. I was given this very set when I was hospitalized for anorexia. I want you to have it." She lets the bags drop to the pavement, then pulls me in for a monstrous hug, whispering, "You're a good person, Gary."

I climb into the back seat before she has another chance to question me. Mom lights up a cigarette before I even get the door shut. Like old times, I roll down the windows, sprinkles of cold rain spitting inside.

Don't say anything about her smoking or you'll hurt—

Is that all the better you can do?

"Mom," I say, asserting my new look, "could I ask you to not smoke until we get home, please. I'd appreciate it."

She turns to me, shocked.

"Mom?"

Now look what you did. You upset—

"Uh, sure, Gary," she replies, coming out of a stupor. "No problem. What is this? My son, Gary, actually being honest with me? I think I can live with this." The corners of her mouth curl up into a happy grin.

"Me too," I reply.

Good job.

Back to the salt mines I go. I feel confident that I can wisely manage my new and improved resources.

We pull into the garage. As Mom turns off the engine, I reach over and touch her forearm, similar to what she did with me upon leaving my Unit 13 room during my first admission—except I don't pull away. Mom freezes.

"Mom?" I say nervously. " I, uh, I just wanted to say thank you for putting up with me over the last few years. I know I've put you guys through a lot of headaches, and I want to tell you that I appreciate everything you've done for me. I, uh, I love you."

Mom briefly revisits her coma-like state, but only for a moment. She looks teary eyed, flushed, and happy. "You're welcome, Gary. Dad and I are very proud of you, regardless of whether or not you have an eating disorder. We love you, too."

Music to my ears. I'm sick of that dumb old *Rambo* soundtrack anyway.

I haul my things into the house one load at a time. Ouch! As I toss a bedpan full of hospital gift store trinkets onto my bed, my big toe sticks into something sharp under my bed—my *Rambo* knife. I reach under and pull it out, staring at it with a deep revulsion. "What a waste of money and time you've been. Why do companies even sell this sort of junk?"

On my final trip to the car to bring in the last box, I pass by our garbage can stationed near the newly constructed foyer Dad slaved over all summer and stop, the knife still in my hand along with a small box of *Sports Illustrated* magazines. A hunger pang nips at my stomach. I crave sugar. I set down the box, reach into my pocket, pull out the cookie Greta gave me after our final Scrabble game, and hold it up opposite my knife.

Toss it out, just like you planned on doing.

My stomach whines for me to send the cookie down its way.

The city garbage truck wheezes to a stop in front of our neighbors' house. Our pickup is next on the route. Dad forgot to set out the garbage on the curb this morning.

I tightly clench the handle of my prized knife. A streak of my own blood still taints the blade's razor sharp edge. The garbage truck's hydraulic crusher whines loudly in the background. If I don't get the garbage can to the curb now, the truck will pass us by. Dad would hate that.

Then pitch the cookie and get the can out there.

The truck pulls in gear and moves ahead.

Pitch it now.

"You know," I mumble out loud, "I think I will, along with this stupid eating disorder," I slam dunk the knife into the garbage can as hard as my arm will allow. I get to the curb just in time.

As I walk back to my box of knickknacks, I peel open the cookie's plastic wrapper and take a big bite. It tastes so good to be free.

You're going to get f—

No, I won't. And if that's all the creative you can get with your comebacks, you'll never make it on the comedy club circuit.

"*Gaa*-ry!" screeches Mom out the kitchen window, observing the truck at our front curb. "Would you hurry and take out the garbage, please?"

In the distance, I hear the hydraulic crusher doing its job. With the rewarding thought of my knife, and the prospect of my eating disorder, being pulverized into a zillion pieces, I yell back to Mom, "I already did!"

Ring, ring... ring, ring... The kitchen phone rings.

Well done, Gary... very well done.

I like this voice. Who are you, really?

YOU, my friend. I am YOU.

"Gary! Telephoooooooooooone! It's Jim Gantner. He wants to check on how you're doing. There's also a letter sitting here for you with red hearts all over it. It says here it's from some girl named Emilee..."

I like what I hear.

EPILOGUE

Many people have asked me if "total" recovery from an eating disorder is truly possible. If what they mean is not dieting any longer, or seeing a "fat" person staring back at me in the mirror, or exercising to extremes, or being obsessed with weight, food, calories and how much "fat" can be pinched at the waist, then yes, I truly believe recovery is doable. It ultimately boils down to growing into an entirely different lifestyle over time. As one of my favorite graduate school professors was fond of saying: "It's a process, process, process."

However, recovery from an eating disorder does not and will not constitute a freedom from the effects of life's inevitable troubles, including my biggest archenemy, shame. To this day, I am still pestered on occasion by this little "voice" in the back of my brain, saying, "You'll never be good enough" or "You always were such an idiot!" when I make a mistake. Scream as it might, an eating disorder no longer decides how I choose to think and behave. I'm a new man with transformed vision, goals, and beliefs.

After my final discharge on December 15, 1989, I made the choice to not pattern my life after old, destructive habits. Over time, I learned to replace them with a healthier lifestyle. It wasn't an overnight cure by any means but a consistent, gradual ascent toward wellness, with lots of minor setbacks along the way. I wrestled with not liking myself for periods after my hospitalizations, but I didn't use obsessive exercise and eating rituals to control my situation. I took on and practiced productive coping strategies that I learned on Unit 13, like: journaling, talking to people I trusted, getting involved in my church and the community, reading and writing, moderate exercise, working outside in the yard, exploring new relationships, striving after career goals, and the like. I attended outpatient therapy with my psychiatrist weekly, then bi-monthly, then once every other month, and eventually once every six months. This helped wean me from three different medications and kept me focused.

Shortly thereafter, Dr. Buckmier and I shook hands for the very last time. It was not only a milestone in my recovery process, but also a tangible reward, reminding me that hard work and persistence really do pay off. I was finally rid of my anorexia lifestyle. I returned to college and finished my degree in Allied Health, reeled in my first professional career as a physical therapy exercise assistant, began dating again, got married, had our first child, completed graduate school, and landed a school counselor position in the public school system—healed and happy, though not perfect. I've learned to embrace the benefits of moderation and balance in just about everything I do. I've accepted my temperament and personality style for what it is and given up my mock game show Let's Be Somebody Else. I've embraced my Christian faith like no other time in my life, making it real and practical. I've gone with the punches, not worrying myself to death over things I cannot control.

I've chosen recovery. So can you.

This book can be used in a clinical setting in many ways. Clients can read it and discuss it with their therapists. Doctors can "prescribe" it to patients en route to a possible inpatient experience. Treatment centers can use it as part of a small group discussion or group therapy sessions with patients. Skinny Boy can also be a source of hope for parents who feel helpless watching their teenage daughter or son quickly sink into self-destructive patterns. Help is available and people do recover from eating disorders.

Depending upon the reader, I recommend "chewing" on the following questions as you read. For those already entrapped in an eating disorder: 1) What do you want? Is it recognition? Courage to grow up? A positive, practical relationship with the Lord? Acceptance for who you are, not what you think others want you to be? Permission to have an identity of your own? Freedom to express genuine emotion? The "guts" to face and accept the hurt of your past and begin a new chapter in your life? 2) What are some realistic steps to get what you want? A large gulping of your pride? Making an appointment with a professional counselor? Forgiving someone who hurt you? Forgiving yourself? Asking someone to help carry your burden for a while? Start journaling? Taking a risk and run a few less miles today and deal with what happens?

If you're a parent of someone with an eating disorder: 1) What expectations do I have for my daughter? Are they realistic, or am I trying to vicariously live out what I want through my son? 2) Do I feel at ease expressing genuine emotion in my daughter's presence? 3) Am I okay with granting my daughter permission to "stretch her wings," or do I feel the need to protect her like a mother bird? 4) When was the last time I hugged my son and told him I'm proud of him (not for what he's accomplished but for who he is)? 5) Have you provided your daughter with support and encouragement while at the same time allowing her to experience the consequences of her own decisions (unless safety is in imminent danger)? 6) How have I embraced his unique personality without trying to break him like a wild horse? 7) How much do I take responsibility for my daughter, constantly attempting to control how she thinks, feels, and acts, instead of being responsible to her?

If you're a friend of someone with an eating disorder, ask yourself: 1) In what ways have I shown my friend that I care? You may want to say, "I don't want to pry into your personal life, but I've noticed you've lost a lot of weight lately, won't hang out with me anymore, and seem distant. Are you okay?" 2) How have I offered assistance to my struggling friend? Options to think about: privately offer a listening ear; offer to go with her to seek help; invited him to a party, athletic event, or social gathering.

When a person's physical health is in imminent danger, it's important to seek immediate professional help, despite the person's adamant refusal. However, for non life-threatening cases, keep in mind that no matter how hard you try, you cannot make a person do something she or he does not want to do. There is a point where you simply need to back off, while at the same time continuing your encouragement and emotional presence. Though it might not make sense, you need to take care of yourself and allow the struggling person to struggle, especially when they approach the older teen years. There's a delicate balance with this and it needs to be handled with sensitivity, respect, intuition, past experiences, and common sense. But overall, it's important to allow the person to feel the pain of poor choices and not have a well-meaning caregiver jump in to the waters of adversity and "save" her. Believe me, she is capable of swimming to shore on her own. Her swimming style may not look pretty, or be exactly like yours, but she'll be back to shore in no time. She needs to learn how to take care of herself and do many things on her own, and that means granting her your blessing to do so. This helps build self-confidence and feels good—for all involved.

ACKNOWLEDGEMENTS

This book would not have been possible if not for a band of exceptional professionals and supportive people.

First and foremost, I'd like to thank my Lord and Savior, Jesus Christ, for His good timing. I am a firm believer in what was ultimately intended to harm me, God intended for good. Without enduring this eating disorder, this "thorn in my side," I might never have discovered the real me or blossomed from my crusty shell.

Close behind is my family: Dad, Mom, Greg, Gina, and Rick. Without your patience and encouragement while I struggled and clawed through my eating disorder searching for a rhyme or reason as to why it was happening to me, I would never have come through the regenerated person I am today.

For my wife, Jeanna, and my kids, Abby, Moriah, and Brant, you are my family now—my team. Thank you for allowing me the time to put this book together. You've been extraordinarily reassuring and "in my corner" the whole time, and I am deeply grateful. I love you each very much.

I am indebted to my Gary Toyn and my publisher American Legacy Media for giving me the chance to live out a dream after countless hours of toil and waiting and literally hundreds of rejection letters. Thank you for your expertise and investment. I look forward to a bright future together.

To Kristen King, my editor, for her impeccable editing skills of wading through a rough manuscript with lots of kinks, cheers to you. You're certainly my pick the next time around.

To the fine folks at ANAD (National Association of Anorexia Nervosa and Associated Disorders) for their dedication and hard work over the years, thank you for sending me opportunities to speak out about the reality of recovery.

To Jim Gantner, not only the best second baseman the Milwaukee Brewers ever had, but a good and honorable man. Thank you for taking the time to visit me in the hospital and making a difference in this young boy's life.

To my two graduating high school classes, I take my hat off to you. Your unwavering support with a young peer, who was terrified of your rejection that never came, is forever etched into my memory. I only wish more high school classes today demonstrated the respect and honor you bestowed to me.

To my good friend and colleague, Merlyn Burkard, who read my first draft and provided insightful feedback and a timely ego boost, thank you. I look forward to many more lunches together.

There are many former patients who sat through group therapy with me day after day, week after week, and witnessed a side of me few have ever seen. Thank you for listening—really listening. I have no idea where Chandra and Emilee are today, but my prayer is that you are safe, healthy, and happy.

From what I understand, many of the remarkable staff on Unit 13, at that time my second "family" who stood tough in the face of my stubbornness and watched me grow, have moved on to bigger and better things. A few of you plead ignorance with how to handle a shy, insecure, teenage boy with anorexia, but your belief in my ability to overcome my plight paid off handsomely. I will never forget your listening ears during desperate nights, your countless pep talks, your unconditional acceptance and tenderness when I considered myself unlovable, and your unique strategies that helped me open the window to my recovery. Your legacy lives on today through my methods of counseling, and hopefully through others who will benefit by them.

For more information about eating disorders, or to contact author Gary Grahl, visit

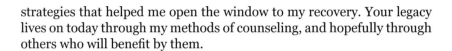

SkinnyBoyBook.com